DISCI-PLESHIP PROJECT

LUCAS LEYS
DAVID NOBOA

COLLEGE MINISTRY

DISCI-PLESHIP PROJECT

LUCAS LEYS
DAVID NOBOA

e625.com

DISCIPLESHIP PROJECT—COLLEGE MINISTRY
e625 - 2024
Dallas, Texas
e625 ©2024 by **Lucas Leys and David Noboa**

_____

All Bible verses are from the New International Version (NIV) unless otherwise specified.

Translated by: Josiah Brown

Interior Design and Cover: JuanShimabukuroDesign

ISBN: 978-1-954149-57-1

PRINTED IN THE UNITED STATES OF AMERICA

CONTENTS

INTRO

*Success is only a consequence of having developed
discipline with perseverance.*

Lucas Leys, *Stamina*

In the Bible we find the story of when Jesus, after his resurrection, had an encounter with two of his disciples while they were walking toward Emmaus, a city located 6 miles from Jerusalem. As we read in this story from Luke chapter 24, those who claimed to be his followers did not know, at that moment, who he was. Doesn't that statement intrigue you? How is it that those who recognized themselves as his followers could not recognize him? The answers can be many. Some illustrate Jesus hidden behind a cloak, others say that his glorified image was different from his human form previous to the crucifixion, or perhaps he had the ability to confuse people's eyes so that they did not recognize him. The truth is that they did not know who he was until the moment he broke the bread and only then could they recognize him.

Whatever the explanation, the story highlights a powerful truth: It is not enough to know who Jesus is. Jesus can walk with you without you being able to recognize him, and suddenly, poof! a great revelation comes into your life that makes you see clearly that Jesus has been walking and talking with you the whole time.

THAT IS THE TASK OF THE DISCIPLERS: WALK WITH SOMEONE SO THEY CAN CLEARLY SEE JESUS.

That is the task of disciplers: walk with someone so that they can clearly see Jesus; accompanying another who still cannot recognize him in certain aspects of their life. And that is the challenge of biblical discipleship: traveling with another person until they can recognize the Messiah, their inner blindfolds drop, and they experience the presence of God through the risen Christ.

WHAT DISCIPLESHIP IS NOT

On many occasions, the clearest way to define something is to list what it is not, and here is a list of what biblical discipleship is not

- **IT IS NOT A BIBLE CLASS.** Usually, these two expressions get confused with each other since they often go hand in hand, but they are not the same. Teaching the Bible is an indispensable part of discipleship and that is why this book contains lessons to teach. However, this book includes the word *project* because just teaching a Bible class is not the whole of discipleship.

- **IT IS NOT A MEMBERSHIP PROGRAM.** In some churches it is believed that discipleship is an initiation program for new believers. We want new believers to start being disciples of Jesus and it is great that there is a good program for those who are taking their first steps in faith. But discipleship does not end with baptism or with the completion of a course. It is not about attending a series of workshops. Although these can help a lot in the discipleship process, you will see that biblical knowledge and other types of learning do not necessarily result in greater spiritual maturity.

- **IT IS NOT A DOCTRINAL REFLECTION.** Discipleship is not limited to intellectual matters. Rather, it is a process of integral character development that involves, in addition to the brain, the spirit, emotions, will, and conduct. Theology classes could make us fall into the delusion that by learning certain doctrines, we will be good disciples. The doctrines, of course, are fundamental and there is doctrinal teaching in true biblical discipleship, but those doctrines must be put into action to have an effect. Knowing theology and doctrine does not make you a good disciple if it does not lead to a tangible practice. Consider, for example, the Pharisees, whom Jesus was confronting. They had a lot of knowledge, and they handled theology and doctrine perfectly, but their hearts were far from God.

GENUINE DISCIPLESHIP IS MORE LIKE BEING A MIRROR OF CHRIST THAN SIMPLY TEACHING ABOUT HIM.

- **IT IS NOT A LITURGY.** Although it is. It is true that discipleship has a lot to do with acquiring good habits and spiritual disciplines, these things should not become cold repetitions or rigid religious behavior. Each discipline acquired, each moment of collective worship, each act of community participation, prayer, and fasting, are tools for our hearts to be conquered by the heart of Jesus and not only for us to "do" what is right in the eyes of others.

One can know a lot about God and be far from him, and because of this, genuine discipleship is more like being a mirror of Christ than simply teaching about him.

The point is not to "show" who is more like Jesus but to be clear that the more I focus on willingly reflecting Christ, the better discipler I will be.

So, what is biblical discipleship? Putting together just one sentence that includes all that genuine discipleship means can be very daring. . . but we can try:

CHRISTIAN DISCIPLESHIP IS A PROCESS OF ACCOMPANIMENT IN WHICH, THROUGH A PERSONAL RELATIONSHIP, SOMEONE IS ABLE TO FACILITATE IN THE DISCIPLE THE VIRTUES OF THE CHARACTER OF JESUS.

THINK OF THESE TWO WORDS

- **PROCESS:** Discipleship is a progressive and patient process. It has to do with accompanying a person from one place to another, just as it happened with the travelers in Emmaus. As they walked, Jesus reminded them of things they had already heard and told them things they did not yet know. And they lived the "process" of that walk with such intensity that when they finally realized it was their Master, they remembered that their hearts burned while he spoke to them.

- **RELATIONSHIP:** Discipleship does not happen without accompaniment. Walking together with someone means "being there" for that person. It's not just about giving lessons or classes, and it needs to be more than just a weekly meeting. Discipleship goes beyond being together for church services or scheduled meetings. The best disciplers share other moments of life with their apprentices and that is why the lessons in this book will challenge you to move from the lesson into community. That's how Jesus did it. And that is how we will do it.

THE MORE I FOCUS ON VOLUNTARILY REFLECTING CHRIST, THE BETTER DISCIPLER I WILL BE.

The twelve disciples were not the only followers of Jesus, but they were the most intimate. Throughout the time that our Messiah walked among human beings, many were close to him and that is still true today. Do you remember the crowd eating freely of the loaves and fishes?

There may be many followers of Jesus, but not all who claim to follow him are truly his disciples.

The Bible says that the Word became flesh and dwelt among us. He lived with men proclaiming that the kingdom of heaven had drawn near. He died. He rose again. And just before leaving to return to the throne prepared for him, he left a great task: *Go and make disciples, teach them to observe all the things that I have told you.* Then it is said that more than 500 people witnessed the ascension of the Savior (1 Corinthians 15:6).

The great task of making disciples of all nations is being carried out with various nuances, and in initiating this project in our churches, the imperative question to answer is: How can we make better disciples of Jesus?

As you go through this book, you will be given 10 crucial premises about the different aspects that biblical discipleship represents. Beyond the transmission of knowledge, these premises are intended to help you in the transmission of a CULTURE. That is what Christ came to establish: the culture of the kingdom of heaven, the precise interpretation of what the Father had said since ancient times, the social exercise of a people, which we now call family, and the characteristics that this family must have. As you can see, these are valuable things that we cannot forget.

Jesus announced that he had come to fulfill the law and not to abolish it, but he did not teach his disciples a series of steps to be better believers. He lived a lifestyle of faith with them. Jesus was with his disciples even in the most difficult moments, but he did not gather them together to give them a talk on obedience. He obeyed the Father in everything, and thus taught them to do the same.

*This is the covenant I will make with them after that
time, says the Lord. I will put my laws in their hearts,
and I will write them on their minds.*

(Hebrews 10:16)

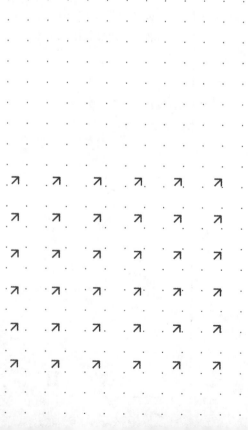

PRIOR TRAINING FOR DISCIPLERS

Your church and ministry can do transformational discipleship and this preliminary training is intended to:

- Break any incorrect paradigm that exists around biblical discipleship in the understanding of your team members.

- Excite and encourage your volunteers with the challenging and wonderful project of making your participants more like Jesus.

- Optimize the growth process by establishing clear results for your ministry.

- Expand the vision of all those involved, recovering the sense of community of the first-century church.

ESSENTIAL PRINCIPLES OF BIBLICAL DISCIPLESHIP

PRINCIPLE 1

WE ARE THE CHURCH

The greatest gift a church can receive is to have a group of families who take their responsibilities with such Christian seriousness that they are willing to completely alter their lifestyle to raise up disciples for Jesus Christ.

Abraham Kuyper

For a long time, we got so used to having meetings in a temple as part of the natural exercise of the church that this inertia produced in us a forgetfulness. We forgot we must be and make disciples, and not just attend meetings. In a biblical sense, the church is not a place to go, but a family to belong to, and if we fail to see it in this way, we will end up stunting our personal growth and that of the church.

The way we speak exhibits how we think and, consequently, how we act. Look at this conversation.

—What church do you go to?

—I attend Central Church.

—But... are you one of those who serve?

— I only attend, I am not in any ministry.

THE CHURCH IS NOT A PLACE TO GO, BUT A FAMILY TO BELONG TO.

Surely you heard something similar. But the truth is that "attending" an ecclesial community is practically impossible from God's perspective. Think of your family.

Do you attend your family weekly or are you part of it? Being part of the church and congregating is not the same as attending.

A biblical answer to the above question would be:

—I do not attend a church; I *am* the church of Christ.

Another very common comment is the following:

—I didn't go to church this week.

And their leader replies: —Well, you shouldn't miss it because remember we shouldn't stop congregating.

Nobody has bad intentions when saying these things but doing so can push the new generations to lead a double life. What exactly is congregate? Obviously, the word means to come together but in a biblical sense it means to be linked. Share a feeling, a belief, and a practical coexistence.

SAYING "WE ARE THE CHURCH" LETS US KNOW THAT WE ARE PART OF THE CHURCH AND WE WILL NEVER STOP BEING SO.

We must avoid having on one side of life: church meetings in which everyone is good, helpful, and even a good example for others, while having on the other side the "secular life." We have lived in that dichotomy for centuries, and it is time to say that it is wrong and that it is not biblical because, according to the written Word, there is no Christian life and secular life. If you are a disciple of Jesus then you are in whatever place, moment, condition, and activity; and everything you do you must do for the Lord (Colossians 3:23-24).

The phrase "go to church" makes us think that it is a destination to visit, a good place to hang out on certain days of the week. Instead, saying "we are the church" lets us know that we are a part of the church, and we never stop being so, no matter where we are or whom we are with.

Look at the following text from your Bible:

> *The God who made the world and everything in it is the Lord of heaven and earth and does not live in temples built by human hands. And he is not served by human hands, as if he needed anything. Rather, he himself gives everyone life and breath and everything else. From one man he made all the nations, that they should inhabit the whole earth; and he marked out their appointed times in history and the boundaries of their lands. God did this so that they would seek him and perhaps reach out for him and find him, though he is not far from any one of us. "For in him we live and move and have our being". As some of your own poets have said, "We are his offspring."*
> (Acts 17:24-28)

God is not always in the temples, but he is always in the church.

Many find it difficult to understand this phrase because they consider the temple as a synonym for church, but it is not. We are the church! What verse 28 says is compelling: "'For in him we live and move and have our being.' As some of your own poets have said, 'We are his offspring.'" God is in the church, so he dwells in us, and we are a part of his family.

GOD IS NOT ALWAYS IN THE TEMPLES, BUT HE IS ALWAYS IN THE CHURCH.

We gather in temples, yes, but God is not there because of the place; he is there because of us, his church. True disciples never cease to be the church and that is precisely why they are aware that they must be an active part of the meetings. They know how important community life is, they are a part of the body, they relate to others, and they serve God with their gifts and talents. But their mission does not end there. The disciple looks inside themself, examines themself periodically, and renders an account to their discipler based on the growth steps that the individual has taken. For this reason, although one participates in the meetings, **a disciple does not depend on the meeting to grow and fulfill what Christ has entrusted to them.**

Attending a congregation does not require you to be a disciple but BEING PART of a community of followers of Jesus requires you to be a disciple wherever you are, and requires you to fulfill the mission of making other disciples! No matter what community of believers you belong to, the mission remains the same, and you remain a part of the global church. We are all united in the same faith, purpose, and mission.

This perspective is born from understanding that the church is not a place limited to a physical space, but is a living organism and, as such, must grow integrally, as well as reproduce, multiply, and expand. If this does not happen, it is because we are doing something wrong.

Remember that just being a disciple of Jesus is not God's complete plan for you. It is also necessary to make disciples, model the character of Christ to others, accompany them to live this process, and encourage them to duplicate themselves in others.

PARADIGM SHIFTS

- I do not attend a church; I AM the church.

- The building where we meet is NOT the church, it is a temple.

- The church is not a static place; it is a LIVING organism.

- The church is made up of the children of God, wherever they come together. Whether that's in a large auditorium, in a park, or in a house, wherever the children of God are, that is where the church is.

IMPLEMENT IDEAS THAT CHANGE THE CULTURE

- Put up posters in the temple with phrases that help everyone change their mindset from "going to church" to "being the church."

- Try to repeat these phrases several times in meetings until the concepts become part of the habitual language.

- Work with all ministry members and volunteers so that in classes, small group meetings, and even individual counseling it is clearly stated that everything we Christians do every day has to do with the church.

PRINCIPLE 2

TEACHING AND DISCIPLESHIP ARE NOT THE SAME THING

A Christian understanding of the world sees a child´s character not as genetically determined but as shaped to a significant degree by parental discipleship and discipline.

Russell D. Moore

It is easy to mix up teaching and discipleship because teaching is part of discipleship, but it is essential to differentiate between them. While discipleship uses teaching, teaching alone does not make disciples.

The practical reality of today's Christians is that we are bombarded by an enormous amount of diverse information, messages, and teachings on multiple networks. We have everything, and we idolize those who "speak better" and have popular social followings, but. . . how are we making disciples? Obviously, we don't want to judge anyone's character, but it's good to be clear that speaking well for a limited amount of time in a video or on a stage is not the same as doing what Jesus commanded us to do. Discipling is more than just speaking well.

Perhaps the key is not to stay in the discursive part of communication. Both authors of this book worked on this material because we want to help you include personal challenges in your teaching and in that intentional process which we are calling discipleship.

The personal or collective challenges that put into practice what has been learned in a relationship optimize results.

Reflect with your team on these differences between teaching and discipleship:

TEACHING	DISCIPLESHIP
Transmits knowledge.	Transmits a culture.
Is limited to classes and does not require much of a relationship with the teacher.	Aims for accompaniment and requires a relationship with the discipler.
Is based on knowing what the Bible or theology says.	Is based on practicing what the Bible says.
Leads you to greater knowledge.	Leads you to maturity in Christ.
Is a short moment or stage of life aimed to finish a program, training, or class.	Is a process that focuses on one's character.

If you pay attention to this chart, you can see that discipleship takes much more effort and time than teaching. Teachers are a key part of the process, but if you really want to disciple others, you are going to have to move to a new level of commitment and relationship. The process can start with teaching, but it doesn't end there.

WHOEVER EXERCISES THE INTENTIONAL PROCESS OF DISCIPLESHIP ASSUMES TRAITS OF SPIRITUAL PATERNITY.

Can you be a teacher and not be making disciples? Yes. When you limit teaching to the imparting of information, then the Word becomes a theory, and that conformism prevents God's truth from being real and alive in the person's life.

When you understand this and change the way you teach, then everything you teach will bear more fruit, since it will point toward the goal of making disciples and not just creating clones that know everything you already know. Additionally, at the end of the road, we are sure that you will be taught by each disciple too, because you never stop being one!

Someone who disciples is much more than a teacher. Little by little they become an example of life, a counselor, a coach, and a friend. Whoever exercises the intentional process of discipleship assumes traits of spiritual paternity since they assign identity, provide, and protect.

PARADIGM SHIFTS

- Teaching is not the "whole point" of discipleship.

- The driving force of discipleship is the relationships, not the knowledge.

- Knowing the Bible does not bring maturity; living it does.

IMPLEMENT IDEAS THAT CHANGE THE CULTURE

- Begin to differentiate biblical classes from discipleship processes.

- Instruct all involved (leaders, volunteers, and participants) to understand the difference.

- Identify those in your congregation who can be disciplers and train them with this guide.

- Make sure that all classes point to changes of action that will be monitored in a relationship.

PRINCIPLE 3

EVERY DISCIPLE IS DIFFERENT

Fortunately, God made all varieties of people with a wide variety of interests and abilities. He has called people of every race and color who have been hurt by life in every manner imaginable. Even the scars of past abuse and injury can be the means of bringing healing to another. What wonderful opportunities to make disciples!

Charles R. Swindoll

The Greek philosophy that we inherited in the West from the Roman Empire gave us the not-so-astute idea that education should be like a funnel through which we all go in differently and then we all come out the same. Some have unknowingly sought this type of approach for discipleship and the church.

For this reason, programs are created with the expectation that every believer can complete them and become the same as all other Christians. However, today it is clear that we are all the same in essence, but we are all unique and we must all be brought to discipleship. Recognizing this is a good thing! Every disciple is different, has specific needs, and struggles with things that others don't. Their strengths and weaknesses are unique, and it is not possible to create a program that can serve everyone equally.

EVERY DISCIPLE IS DIFFERENT, HAS SPECIFIC NEEDS, AND STRUGGLES WITH THINGS THAT OTHERS DON'T.

In turn, the disciplers are aware of their own weaknesses in order to depend more on Christ, assume their strengths to be imparted to their followers, and are all fully guided by the Spirit of God.

It is for this reason that discipleship is more about personal development than just a collective group development. The group and the individual must be two complementary parts because it is not one or the other but both. There are truths that are better learned communally and others that must be taught face-to-face in the intimacy of two people. The challenge is that almost all church programs are made up of a big or small collective of people and there is little one-on-one approach. This is why it is so vital to remember that intimate conversations, personal encounters, and one-on-one challenges are a mark of genuine discipleship.

Some ideas to disciple on a personal level:

- Don't look at numbers, look at people.

- Create opportunities that go outside of a class setting.

- Create appropriate intentional intimacy as opposed to waiting for it to come naturally.

- Find out the interests of each disciple.

- If you want a genuine relationship, be authentic.

- Invest more into those who show greater interest and enthusiasm.

- Teach them to be accountable for their lives. This is imperative.

- Celebrate their successes; comfort them in their setbacks.

- Work on specific actions.

- Help them set/focus on personal goals.

- Assist them in depending on the Holy Spirit to be their guide.

These tips will vary slightly if you are discipling children, preteens, teens, or young adults. Each of the following principles will assist you in discovering the superior point of focus for each of the age groups. There is, however, no age limitation for someone to become a disciple.

PARADIGM SHIFTS

- To God we are all equal, but we are also different and unique.

- Discipleship always becomes a personal relationship.

- The weekly meetings do not disciple; the relationship does.

- We were created in the image and likeness of a multiform God.

IMPLEMENT IDEAS THAT CHANGE THE CULTURE

- Know the individual differences of the people who are in your discipleship group.

- Intentionally be aware of which paradigm is important to transfer value to them.

- Help the people you disciple get to know each other better.

- Create a conscious awareness of inclusion and integration in the members of your discipleship projects.

- Model a personalized pastoral approach.

PRINCIPLE 4

DISCIPLESHIP IS FOR EVERY AGE

Jesus spent time and had close and personal relationships with his disciples. Do we have personal relationships with the new generations in our churches?

La Verne Tolbert

It seems that the general conscience of many congregations demands that we "seriously" disciple adults, while children, preteens, teens, and young adults can wait, and this is a strategic error with dire consequences. In fact, when it comes to transmitting culture, the best age is the youngest. When you work with adults you will find that it is a little more difficult to change something that they have done in a certain and determined way for their entire lives. Instead, the youngest are moldable, teachable, and adaptable. They know that they don't know, and that's good.

If you have an influential position with the new generations, God has held you in high esteem.

Now, working with children is not the same as working with young adults, so here are some recommendations that correspond to the 4 basic work areas of an intelligent vision for generational pastoral care.

> **WHEN IT COMES TO TRANSMITTING CULTURE, THE BEST AGE IS THE YOUNGEST.**

FOR THE DISCIPLESHIP OF CHILDREN

- Work closely with parents. They are the natural leaders and disciplers that God gave children. Discipling children is cooperating with their parents.

- Help children share their growth steps in the context of their family.

- Use multiple sources, so the training process will be comprehensive and will reach everyone. (If you want to know more about multiple intelligences, take advantage of the course at the e625 online Institute.)

FOR THE DISCIPLESHIP OF PRETEENS

- This is the stage where we begin to see the world beyond just the home and with the arrival of abstract thought we begin to question the validity of what we learned in childhood. For this reason, teaching must move from concrete data to abstract principles.

- At this stage it is also crucial to collaborate with their parents because this is the last great opportunity they will have to shape desired values and habits in their children. In the following stages of their lives, instilling values becomes more difficult.

- The relationship with their leaders and teachers must now be more personal. They need models and it is very possible that the models they have at this stage will continue to subconsciously be their example for the rest of their lives.

FOR THE DISCIPLESHIP OF TEENS

- The relationship of boys and girls with their parents is always important, but the relationship with their friends at this age is key. Communal discipleship is most significant at this stage.

- Naturally, in adolescence we all question our family framework and leaders should not throw more fuel on the fire but rather help them positively make that evaluation.

- Be prepared to talk with them about feelings and emotions. Their life during this stage is going to be a roller coaster of emotional ups and downs and they will need someone mature, and therefore stable, to accompany them.

FOR THE DISCIPLESHIP OF YOUNG ADULTS

- To the same degree that communal discipleship is vital in the previous stage, mentorship is vital in this young adult phase. A mentor meets their deepest needs and allows space to ask difficult questions, even the most intimate questions.

- Present options to young adults without giving them orders and, above all, without making decisions for them. Teach them to make their decisions based on the Word of God. Coaching is a good discipline to add to your skills and in the e625.com online institute you can find foundational generational coaching courses.

- In this stage, most consider pursuing a profession, choosing a marriage partner, planning for the future, and discovering one's life purpose (or even a ministerial calling). These are the talking points in the discipleship relationship with young adults.

PARADIGM SHIFTS

- Age is not a limitation to making disciples, but it is necessary to adapt according to the stage.

- Discipling adults is not more valuable than discipling little ones.

- The transferring of culture takes time, focus, and effort.

IMPLEMENT IDEAS THAT CHANGE THE CULTURE

- Work on a vision of *Generational Leadership*.[1] (If you haven't read this book we recommend you do so as soon as possible.) Join the adult ministries with those in your congregation who are dedicated to the new generations and plan an activity that focuses on making the discipleship of new generations a priority for your entire church, as it was commissioned by God in Deuteronomy 6. Coordinating efforts from time to time does wonders for the heart and minds of co-laborers.

- Organize things in a way that each of the new generational stages leads a meeting one or more times per year. Give preteens responsibilities, encourage teens to be an example for the little ones, train young adults to model behavior in teens, and provide examples of maturity to take firm steps toward the next stage in which they find themselves.

---

1. Lucas Leys, *Liderazgo Generacional.* (Dallas, Texas: Editorial e625, 2017).

34

DISCIPLESHIP HAPPENS IN PROCESSES

When the church becomes an end in itself, it ends.
When any ministry, no matter how great, becomes an
end goal, it ends. What we need is for discipleship to
become the goal, and then the process of conversion and
sanctification will never end.
Robby Gallaty

When we talk about discipling others, we must consider how to elevate our disciples' level of maturity. It is about going from one point to the next. This makes it necessary to draw a route that marks the steps of that sustained growth that we seek, while understanding that there are smaller steps along the way. When we understand this better, we focus less on our own assessment of events and pay more attention to a progressive view of processes.

It is one thing to learn a principle and quite another to live it. The first is an intellectual act, something that can be received in a class. To put a principle into practice, however, requires decision, effort, and the fulfillment of goals that help make the principle a part of our culture and way of life.

For this reason, someone who decides to disciple cannot be satisfied with teaching principles, since that is only the first part. It is necessary that these principles

WE FOCUS LESS ON OUR OWN ASSESSMENT OF EVENTS AND PAY MORE ATTENTION TO A PROGRESSIVE VIEW OF PROCESSES.

are part of the discipler's culture so that they can transmit them in such a way that they become part of the culture of the disciple.

It is a lifestyle that should arise naturally and not be forced.

THE PENTAGON OF LEARNING APPLIED TO DISCIPLESHIP

The book *Generational Leadership* describes the need to improve teaching methods from a relational nuance with the following pentagon:

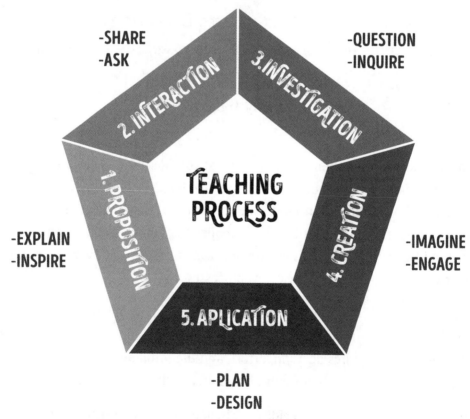

-SHARE
-ASK

-QUESTION
-INQUIRE

2. INTERACTION

3. INVESTIGATION

1. PROPOSITION

TEACHING PROCESS

4. CREATION

-EXPLAIN
-INSPIRE

-IMAGINE
-ENGAGE

5. APLICATION

-PLAN
-DESIGN

© 2017 Lucas Leys

Each one of the sides of the pentagon marks a dimension of the action that the disciplers must observe. If you think about it well, you will understand the need to make disciples through processes, instead of just having students in a class.

Here's an example of how this process works:

1. **PROPOSITION:** Pick an aspect of the character of Christ.

2. **INTERACTION:** Explore the different appreciations of the aspect.

3. **INVESTIGATION:** Look up what the Bible says about it.

4. **CREATION:** Engage others in doing it together.

5. **APLICATION:** Live it in your own flesh and be accountable for it.

A process can be focused on a specific area of the disciple's life, on a specific theme, on an aspect of character, etc., In this way you can create different proposals for stages that adapt to the principles of this pentagon. Nothing is rigid. On the contrary, everything is adaptable and 100 percent improvable and you can read more in the book *Generational Leadership*.

Although this book may appear to speak to the project of making disciples, it is meant as a tool to help guide a long-term process whose final goal is to form the character of Christ in the life of the believer, which is entirely dependent on the relationship between discipler and disciple and their mutual commitment to the process.

PARADIGM SHIFTS

- Discipleship is not a propositional discourse but a process of internalizing truths that respect the different abilities of our brains to learn.

- The preacher shares a monologue, the teacher teaches a class, the discipler accompanies through stages.

- The relationship between disciplers and disciples is the very nature of discipleship.

IMPLEMENT IDEAS THAT CHANGE THE CULTURE

- Get used to creating processes. Preaching or lectures are not as effective in generating understanding for most people. Use series, long-term lessons, and various instances so that different people internalize the contents of what you want them to practice.

- The call is not to have meetings where we stand to sing and then listen to a lecture. Think outside the sanctuary, the classroom, and the speeches given.

PRINCIPLE 6

ACCOMPANIMENT AND MENTORSHIP

I believe in the transforming power of the Spirit of God and that Jesus can be formed in the life of the new generations. I work from his reality, not from fiction.
Félix Ortiz

According to what we can notice in the New Testament, the apostle Paul would come to a city, preach, and then continue working with a few select believers until he formed in them the character of Christ so that they would then do the same with others. When it was time, he left there but he did not disconnect from them: he continued to give them instructions through his writings.

If we are talking about relationships and processes, we must consider the development of relationships in phases or stages and that is why it is good to include the word project. If we want to form disciples with maturity, who truly reflect the character of Christ, we must first form the attributes of Christ in ourselves and then gradually develop each aspect of our personal commitments, modeling them in the lives of others. Paul said: "Be imitators of me, just as I am of Christ" and this can take years. At the same time, it is advisable to plan it with phases and times, and then release the disciples so that they go and repeat the process with others.

THE GREATEST WEALTH OF DISCIPLESHIP IS IN THE RELATIONSHIP.

The relationship with your disciples can last a lifetime, and they may even perceive you as a spiritual reference, but that does not necessarily mean that the roles are forever and that they will not grow past it. The point is to accompany them in this stage to help them take steps toward maturity they need to take in this period in which they find themselves. This "staying in touch" can use digital tools such as video chats, social media, and similar tools. But the point is to mentor, that is, model to transfer certain vital lessons that must be learned at a stage in life.

Look what the book of Exodus says about God's relationship with Moses. Although Moses could not look directly into the face of God because he would have died, his personal encounter with the Eternal God produced in him a weight of glory that others could not fail to recognize.

> *The Lord would speak to Moses face to face, as one speaks to a friend. Then Moses would return to the camp, but his young aide Joshua son of Nun did not leave the tent.*
> (Exodus 33:11)

In other words, being close to a good role model has an impact that sooner or later everyone will notice. Moses was discipled by God, just as all of us can be. This process is based on the relationship we reach with him. In the same way, we can all accompany others in their growth process.

PARADIGM SHIFTS

- There is no discipleship without accompaniment.

- The greatest wealth of discipleship is in the relationship.

- The discipleship relationship can last a lifetime, although roles usually change according to the stages of life.

IMPLEMENT IDEAS THAT CHANGE THE CULTURE

- Take personal time with each person you have in a discipleship group.

- Let the people in your group know aspects of your life that are outside of a weekly class.

- They should keep in mind from early on that one day they will have to disciple others. Thus, the change will not be left alone in your hands, since the responsibility of making disciples belongs to all believers.

- Create dscipleship projects for specific stages of life with measurable results.

PRINCIPLE 7

PARENTS' INVOLVEMENT

We discipline our children not so that they will make us happy, but so that they will serve Christ as adults. We educate them not so they can have a good job, but to develop them to be the best follower of Jesus that they can be.
Chap Bettis

All Christian parents are involved in the discipleship of their children even if they don't know it or are unintentional about it. The job of every church leader is to make sure parents know this and help them to be intentional about doing it better.

As children grow, their ability and need to relate to other role models also grows. That is where we come in, not as something parallel to the family but rather by joining forces in a collaborative way. The point is that a constant interaction between leadership and parents goes much further than we might suspect. The role of the parents decreases as the children grow older and it is necessary for this to happen, because otherwise, they could never become mature children who effectively serve the kingdom of heaven. But again. . . this is a PROCESS. It could be slow moving, and we must be patient, but that is why, when we work

ALL CHRISTIAN PARENTS ARE INVOLVED IN THE DISCIPLESHIP OF THEIR CHILDREN EVEN IF THEY DON'T KNOW IT

on discipleship from the perspective of the church, we need to nurture a positive relationship with parents as well.

The role of each one could vary over time, in this way:

6–9	10–13	14–17	18–25
• Children are discipled by their parents.	• Parents are important role models, as are leaders and teachers.	• Parents model.	• Parents and leaders delegate autonomy.
• Parents are the clearest role model.	• Parents should get other adults to support their work.	• Leaders are mentors.	• Leaders must be life mentors and coaches for specific decisions.
• Leaders support parents' leadership.	• Their contact with positive teens is vital.	• Parents should relate with their children's friends.	• Contact with young married couples with good relationships is vital.
• Their contact with preteens is vital.		• Contact with young adults who are good role models is vital.	

PARADIGM SHIFTS

- The role of parents changes as the ages advance.
- Leaders without the parents can't get very far.

- The parents must learn to lean on leaders.

IMPLEMENT IDEAS THAT CHANGE THE CULTURE

- Set a good pace for parent meetings based on the age of your students.

- Promote parent-child meetings more often. The interaction that this produces rescues God's design for the church.

- As a disciple, you must always think of each disciple within a family context. There will always be people close to you who can be a good influence on the development of the one you are discipling.

- Let non-Christian parents know that the church is there to help them in their parenthood.

THE MIRROR PRINCIPLE

Discipleship is the process of becoming who Jesus would be if He were you.
Dallas Willard

The apostle John made this principle clear: "Whoever claims to live in him must live as Jesus did" (1 John 2:6).

The first great commitment of those of us who dedicate ourselves to the discipleship project is to reflect Christ in everything: his character, passion, decisions, will, and transparency. That is why it is said that no one can disciple if they are not a disciple first. Anyone who is willing to be a disciple tries to look more like Jesus every day since he came, in turn, to reflect the Father. As Paul says, Christ is the image of the invisible God (Colossians 1:15).

The second great commitment is to extend this for others to also resemble Jesus. For this reason we have an exciting and enormous responsibility that can sometimes intimidate us, for which we must also learn from Jesus's dependence on God. In John 15:15 we find him saying: "I no longer call you servants, because a servant does not know his master's business. Instead, I have called you friends, for everything that I learned from my Father I have made known to you."

How good to know that we have a great and powerful God and that he continually renews his mercy for us because we will need it in this process. If we depend on him in the discipleship project, we will surely succeed!

If you think about it, you will see that creation has that same design. Everything that God created has his stamp of ownership. Everything resembles him. Everything was made by him, through him, and for him. Genesis tells the story of the creation of the human being, saying that they were made "in the image and likeness of God" That is, they were created as a mirror that reflects him and starting from this principle, we could design a discipleship process as follows:

1. I know one aspect of the character of Christ. For example: love.

2. I long to be like him in that way.

3. I stop loving my way, to start loving as he loved.

4. I battle against the arguments that prevent me from loving as he loved.

5. I live and practice his love.

6. I teach others to love like him.

7. I choose another aspect of Christ's character to imitate. And so the whole process begins again.

In this way, the discipleship process will last a lifetime, because in each aspect we can find a new depth in the next stage. It is good to be able to work on it with those we have been put in charge of.

PARADIGM SHIFTS

- Reflecting Jesus in our own lives is more important than giving a good sermon or class about Jesus. That means dying to myself so that he can live in me.

- All creation was made in the image of God, and we must and can recover that design.

- Reflecting Christ is not a feeling or a romantic lyric to a cute song but a concrete action in which you model his character.

IMPLEMENT IDEAS THAT CHANGE THE CULTURE

- Choose specific aspects of Jesus's character to reflect on, understand, and develop.

- Prepare a progressive and ordered teaching plan. Put up signs that say something like: "This is the month of love." You can use videos and images for this purpose, and testimonies can be given about experiences of giving and receiving love, so that everyone involved in the discipleship project is clear about the tangible objective that is being worked on.

REFLECTING CHRIST IS NOT A FEELING OR A ROMANTIC LYRIC TO A CUTE SONG BUT A CONCRETE ACTION IN WHICH YOU MODEL HIS CHARACTER.

ACTIVITIES WITH A PURPOSE

Renewing ourselves is not a luxury, it is a necessity for every follower of Jesus in order to continue being agents of restoration and reconciliation in a broken world.

Félix Ortiz

When we mentally leave behind the sanctuary, the classroom, and the liturgy, our panorama expands to the point that we find new scenarios and possibilities to achieve the great purpose of discipleship, which is that the people we influence become more like Jesus.

For the best disciplers, everything is done with a purpose, both relationships and spontaneous conversations at every available opportunity, as well as good programs that facilitate the internalization of desired behaviors.

Some of these activities will be personal or relationship building for a small group. Others, however, should include the community. This is how we teach kids, pre-teens, teens, and young adults to be one body. There character problems will also be revealed, and they will learn to support each other. Then, the disciples will be aware of the reactions of the disciplers to continue forming Christ in them, and the disciplers will also keep an eye as the disciples to imitate them. In those situations, you will realize that they look at you more than you realize.

Remember that it is not about creative ideas just to be creative, or spectacular activities with the desire to be spectacular. From the point of view of the disciple, even the spectacle of a program is simply a pedagogical tool (and not for

LET US ASK GOD FOR WISDOM TO ENSURE THAT EACH ACTIVITY ALIGNS WITH HIS INTENTIONS FOR OUR MINISTRIES.

you to show off). The basic objectives are to promote coexistence, create interest, and facilitate practical lessons in which to model principles.

Think of all these activities from the perspectives of the purpose of discipleship and you will find a new dimension to them:

- Going for a walk outside

- Playing sports

- Climbing a mountain

- Going swimming

- Planting or caring for a tree or plant

- Reading a book

- Visiting the sick, elderly, or orphans

- Watching a movie

- Going to the theater, circus, dance, etc.

- Carrying out a carpentry project

- Playing or singing a song that you can discuss together

- Visiting a relative

The possibilities are endless.

Let us ask God for wisdom to ensure that each activity aligns with his intentions for our ministries.

PARADIGM SHIFTS

- Exercise, play, and fellowship are excellent ministry tools when done with a purpose.

- The activities planned outside the sanctuary are as rich and necessary as those that take place inside.

- Discipleship is not reduced to listening, but disciples must see and act. That is why it is necessary to create these moments with our programs.

IMPLEMENT IDEAS THAT CHANGE THE CULTURE

- Plan for the long term and share the plan with everyone you can.

- Present a public report of all the activities you facilitate outside the sanctuary. It is always better when everyone finds out about the riches that are achieved in personal discipleship.

- Insistently convey to everyone involved in your ministry the idea that your mission is not for them to listen to a biblical proposition quietly and just say amen. It promotes a culture of coexistence, actions, and experiences and not only of sermons and classes.

THE CALL IS FOR EVERYONE

Discipleship is not a choice.
Tim Keller

To think that only pastors have the call to disciple others is nonsense. The great commission to go and make disciples (Matthew 28:16-20; Mark 16:14-18; Luke 24:36-49; John 20:19-23) was given to all the disciples.

If we acknowledge Jesus as our Lord and Savior, then we have a call to discipleship.

All Christians must disciple and doing so is one of the most tremendous ways we can grow because we all learn by teaching. We have all received something that we can give and have learned something that we can teach. Along the way, some are filled with fear or justifications, thinking that they must prepare a lot or that they could make a mistake. But the reality is that we are all in the process of learning because we never stop being disciples, and of course we are going to make mistakes. That is neither something new, nor is it a tragedy.

If Christ trusts us for this task, it must be because we can do it.

If the church continues to believe that one sermon is enough to make disciples, then we will continue to see burnt-out pastors and continue to turn good preachers into celebrities because they speak well, even if they don't help us achieve what God wants us to achieve. God wants disciples and not people with good

IF WE ACKNOWLEDGE JESUS AS OUR LORD AND SAVIOR, THEN WE HAVE A CALL TO DISCIPLESHIP.

morals and some biblical knowledge to behave like Christians in the temple on the weekend.

Disciples.

The sermons, the songs, and the temple are tools and not objectives and when they are used well, they help us to produce disciples of Jesus. And the great news is that there are other tools and mechanisms modeled by Jesus himself to achieve it.

This is where the most important action of all appears: being a model. Modeling is something that adults and even young adults always do for the new generations even if we are not aware that we are doing it. The entire proposal of Generational Leadership is linked to this reality and invites us to be intentional with it. All Christian adults are involved in the discipleship of the youth although perhaps without knowing it. The young adults are ready to disciple the teens because they are already modeling for them what the next stage is all about and the teens, in turn, are doing the same with the preteens and the preteens are being watched by the kids. Modeling is a natural process, and it is much more effective when we are aware of it and do it with devotion, wit, and fidelity.

PARADIGM SHIFTS

- Discipleship is the task of all God's children.

- Pastors and leaders who do not move everyone to disciple sooner or later will burn out or become superficial, or both.

- Discipleship is something that we may already be doing without realizing it, but that we can improve exponentially if we start doing it intentionally.

IMPLEMENT IDEAS THAT CHANGE THE CULTURE

- The importance of discipleship must be communicated privately, publicly, and continually.

- Delegate authority and don't just focus on your work team and volunteers.

- Celebrate what God celebrates and not what the world already celebrates (such as fame, recognition, beauty, or eloquence).

- Involve new generations in ministry and discipleship at an early age. They are already looking at us.

10 LESSONS FOR DISCIPLING COLLEGE STUDENTS

Discipleship is a call to an exciting adventure. It is also a great challenge: we must strive with all our strength to give the disciples the necessary tools so that they never get stuck in religious inertia. With this in mind, the following lessons are designed with a sequence that we will call "STRIDE," since it gives an idea of movement.

The sequence or model STRIDE is the process that you can see developed in the following acrostic:

 See your environment

 Train together

 Ruminate on a model

 Illuminate yourself with the truth

 Deny yourself

 Emulate the call

As you will see, each action that makes up the acrostic leads us one step forward in the discipleship project. The STRIDE model facilitates a discipleship process in which both the teacher and the learner are challenged to grow and mature.

Here are the details for each step:

1. **See your environment**. This has to do with evaluating the biblical and current context. Looking at what is happening around us gives us guidelines to know what ground we are treading on and to be able to make appropriate decisions based on that context.

2. **Train together.** This section offers a general understanding of the topic and creates the opportunity for the teacher to make an emotional connection, either by telling a testimony or by explaining why they think the topic is important on a personal level.

3. **Ruminate on a model.** There are always protagonists. People who, depending on the topic, will be analyzed and used as a reference. Someone who was successful in the proposed topic, so we can learn from their example.

4. **Illuminate yourself with the truth.** Here the foundation is laid in the Word of God. It is not that it has not been located there before, since each part of the material has been the result of an intentional analysis of the Word of God, but here, all the attention will be placed on some texts of Scriptures to take the learners deeper, and to put the truths into practice.

5. **Deny yourself.** There is nothing wiser and more precious than doing God's will, but there is always a price. That price often includes dying to selfishness, fear, comfort, or the opinions of others.

6. **Emulate the call.** This last part points to the future, establishing steps to take further and contemplating the challenges that the discipler and the disciple will face to bring heaven to earth.

Note that this sequence can also be used to create other topics and lessons or enhance the that are accessible other materials on e625.com.

The one who leads the discipleship (you!) must study the lesson and delve into it to later determine the treatment you want to give each step. Some topics will be hotter and more urgent, depending on the disciples' context, so some lessons could last one, two, or three weeks, depending on what you, your team, and the Holy Spirit dictate.

Yes.

It will be essential for each discipler to walk in a close relationship with the Holy Spirit so that they can be guided by him and thus impact a new generation of disciples.

WARNING

From here we assume that you have already given the principles of biblical discipleship in Session 1 a careful read, and that all members of your team have gone through prior tactical training before starting the lessons that begin below.

Remember that parents are the first persons called to disciple their children, so it's not a bad idea for you to start this material with a mini training for them, or at least with a presentation informing them that you will share the following lessons of this discipleship project with their children.

This project tries to mobilize more people to take up the challenge of not continuing to sit in religious comfort, but to help the generations that come next, inside and outside the meetings or sanctuaries.

LESSON 1

THE GOSPEL IS COUNTERCULTURAL

The world is not our enemy; it is our mission field.
Alex Sampedro, *Craftsman*

The gospel forces us to be countercultural. It requires us to manifest a lifestyle different from the usual parameters of the world. This battle causes many young adults to succumb, turning them into deserters of their own convictions and converting them into followers of the culture that society offers them. We can't let that keep happening!

THE BIG QUESTION WE MUST ANSWER WITH THIS LESSON IS:

How can we remain faithful believers in a world that questions faith?

Living a countercultural gospel does not mean that we are against the world that God loves, but it does mean that we have a mission regarding that world: to transform it. Or rather, return it to the perfect design with which God created it in the beginning. On the other hand, we are in open battle with the forces in culture that distance God from people's thoughts. **Culture moves toward a world without God, while we move with God to transform the world's culture.**

"SANCTUARY CHRISTIANITY" HAS CAUSED US TO LOSE INFLUENCE IN OUR SOCIETY.

"Sanctuary Christianity" has caused us to lose influence in our society. We have created imaginary bubbles that keep the believers from being salt and light as we should, nor does it allow the lost to enter that space to receive light or flavor from Jesus.

Statistics reveal that a large number of young adults drop out of the church right out of high school. It seems that the world gives them better answers than the ones they get inside the church. David Kinnaman puts it this way in his book *You Lost Me*:

"There is a generation of young Christians who believe that the church in which they were raised is not a safe place to have reasonable doubts. Many of them have received prefabricated and superficial answers to their rugged and honest questions from the church; and they are openly rejecting the speeches and opinions that they have seen in the older generations."

It's true! We compete with the excess of freedoms the world offers them, and the few answers we do give them are not enough to keep them firm in their faith. All is not lost, however. We have the keys to an abundant life.

The Word of God is our banner. In addition to knowing it or reciting it, we can live it, and for that to happen we must make it a part of us. Paul tells the Ephesians that faith is the only requirement for salvation, and John tells us in his first letter that faith is the victory that overcomes the world. But the Lord, speaking to Jeremiah, tells him:

> *Therefore this is what the Lord says: "If you repent, I will restore you that you may serve me; if you utter worthy, not worthless, words, you will be my spokesman. Let this people turn to you, but you must not turn to them.*
> **Jeremiah 15:19**

We need to live out our faith, and let our faith be our culture. And if God says it's possible, it's because it is possible! Being influential in the world should be one of the great goals of every disciple. The idea is not to live inside a bubble to protect one from being contaminated, but to infect the world with the grace of the gospel!

◈ SEE YOUR ENVIRONMENT

What is the state of the world in which our young adults live? To disciple young adults in a timely manner, it is necessary to observe the factors that surround them. And it's time to get your young adults to take a hard look at the culture around them, too. The university they attend, the friends they have, and the social habits of their family and environment.

Remember that much of your work as a discipler will come out of the relationship you have with those you are discipling, rather than what you do or say while you are in front of the whole group teaching them.

SOME ADVICE

- Dedicate some time to learn about the reality of your youth. When talking with them, encourage them to name the values they identify around them.

- Ask open questions that give you enough information about their environment.

- Consider meeting their friends and discovering the value each disciple places on them.

- Visit their house, meet their family.

- Dedicate yourself to getting to know each disciple and the factors that surround them, and avoid the temptation to give advice, make value judgments, or worse, lecture them on what they say. This is a time to focus on seeing and knowing their environment.

All this will allow you to have a clearer vision of the battles that each one of them is experiencing. Knowing what career a young adult is studying for and their motivations for doing it, will give you clues about what they think and believe about life and how to function in it. Getting to know their friends will enable you to see what they value in their friends and will be a key indication of the influence they receive on a day-to-day basis. Visiting his or her house, in addition to providing you with valuable information about their environment, will show their parents and siblings that you are interested in them as a person, and not just as another number in the church. Then, when you talk to each disciple, help them put everything you have observed on a scale. Avoid telling them everything that you see wrong in their friends or family as a starting point, or you will lose their trust. Only use questions that help them reflect on what they are doing and why they are doing it. Here are some suggestions:

- Are your friends the kind of people you can learn and grow from?

- Do your parents know your friends and the places you visit?

- Are the practices of the people around you positive or negative? Consider their social habits, their ways of speaking and thinking, etc.

- What do the other people around you think and how do they act, such as classmates, work colleagues, and other acquaintances?

As a discipler, you will come across different cases. Believers, and nonbelievers' parents, believers, and nonbelievers' friends, careers with a high level of humanistic philosophy, and diverse environments that can generate different ways of thinking and acting. This initial exploration will help you to understand the opportunities and threats present in the culture that surrounds the young adults with whom you are going to work.

🎵 TRAIN TOGETHER

All human beings move within a certain culture. Throughout history, each society has experienced milestones that have marked it, for better or worse, transforming the lifestyle of its inhabitants. Each era has its positive and negative aspects.

Along with this, Christians have the Bible, which is our map of life. Most of the time, what Scripture recommends is contrary to what society promotes, and that is when we find the "countercultural effect" of our faith.

The first step is to balance what society says and what the Word of God says. The culture of a disciple of Jesus is rooted in the Bible, and we need to find a way to live according to those parameters without giving in to the demands of a culture contrary to God.

WHAT TODAY'S CULTURE SAYS	WHAT SCRIPTURE SAYS
Live wildly	Live wisely
Practice free sexuality	Guard your purity
Honor yourself and use others	Honor your parents and love your neighbor
Accumulate things	Use your time well
Gender is a social construct that you should use for your pleasure	Gender is designed by God for your fulfillment and that of others
You are the center of the world (egocentric view)	Jesus is the center of everything (Christocentric view)
Religion is a straitjacket	The truth sets you free
Don't care about others	Love your neighbor as yourself

Live and let live	Live to be the salt and light of the world
Protecting my convenience is the best option (for example, with abortion)	Protecting life is always the best option

What the Word of God says is greater than what the world says, but it is necessary to find the foundation for each of the practices and principles of the Bible, and thus be able to have adequate answers to give to the world. The challenge will be how to make your young adults not only listen to the truth contained in the Bible, but learn it, assimilate it, consider it true, welcome it, live it, and teach it to others. Discipleship, then, will depend on finding a way to inject the essence of the Word of God into those who come after, not as a restrictive method to repress the human being but as the greatest proof of God's love, manifested in the instructions that He gave to care for us.

RUMINATE ON A MODEL

You can read this story with your youth in a meeting (or send them a file with the text in advance to read at home or to discuss in a group chat).

MARTIN LUTHER KING JR.

Martin Luther King Jr. was a Baptist pastor who was a world-renowned personality in the twentieth century for his fight against racial and social discrimination. For this man it was not enough to have studied sociology and theology; he was a voracious learner and continued his education until obtaining a doctorate. He had everything needed to lead a comfortable, quiet life, but instead he decided to accept the responsibility of pastoring Dexter Avenue Baptist Congregation in Alabama when he was barely 25 years old. It was the year 1954, and barely a year later he refused to close his eyes to the suffering that was happening around him.

The trigger that turned his outrage into activism against racial profiling was the arrest of a black woman for refusing to give up her seat to a white man. We can imagine that scene. Rosa Parks travels on a bus and manages to sit in a free seat; shortly after, a white man gets on the bus and the driver, noticing that there are no more free seats, demands that Rosa give up her seat, but she refuses to do so. Amid a society that believed that white people were superior to black people, a black woman who refused to give her seat to a white man was considered to have committed a crime. We imagine the indignation of the woman at being arrested and the outrage in the soul of Martin Luther King Jr. upon hearing the story. He couldn't just sit around doing nothing! So he decided to use his intellectual training as a sociologist, and his spiritual influence as a pastor, to battle against injustice. A fight that many thought would be fruitless since society would not change overnight. However, this became a historic fight.

King's decision to stop being a bystander in the face of injustice catapulted many black men and women to speak up, a right that had been taken away from them. Now they had found someone who not only understood them but was willing to be a spokesperson calling for change in a situation that was already untenable.

Conflicts, constant segregation, closed doors, frustration, and tears surrounded their struggle, but the voice of Martin Luther King Jr. traveled through the streets of his city, the country, and the entire world. His "I Have a Dream" speech continues to be remembered and quoted to this day, because although we say that we live in a fairer and less discriminatory society, those wishes have not yet been entirely fulfilled.

The world celebrated with him when he received the Nobel Peace Prize at the age of 35, but later mourned his loss when James Earl Ray murdered him at the age of 39.

And yes, opposing a corrupt, unfair, unbalanced, and oppressive system is exactly what Jesus called us to do. For this we must seek justice, love mercy, and walk humbly before a sovereign God. Perhaps not all of us can be public activists in an urgent struggle as Martin Luther King Jr. was, but we can be the spokespersons for a generation that continues to need men and women who do not conform to what the world says and offers, but who are willing to rescue that world from the clutches of impunity, injustice, and lack of love. People who go against what the culture promotes, against what society thinks, and who are in tune with what their Lord says. This path is not an easy one, but it is the right one.

📖 ILLUMINATE YOURSELF WITH THE TRUTH

It's time to go to the Word of God.

READ THE FOLLOWING VERSES TOGETHER

Enter through the narrow gate. For wide is the gate and broad is the road that leads to destruction, and many enter through it. But small is the gate and narrow the road that leads to life, and only a few find it.
Matthew 7:13-14

AND NOW ASK THE FOLLOWING QUESTIONS

- What do you think this text means?

- In this text, what do you think is the difference between the gate and the road?

- In what ways can we stay on the narrow road?

FOR YOUR REFLECTION

In this passage, Jesus is finishing what we know as the Sermon on the Mount. After talking about the beatitudes, adultery, divorce, love of enemies, prayer, fasting, and judging others, Jesus ends the process by talking about the two gates and the two roads. Then he will say how we will be known by the fruits we bear, and that we will be wise if we build our lives on the rock (him).

If you look closely, Jesus is not just the rock; he is also the gate (John 10:9), and he is also the way (John 14:6). Christ is everything, and more! He is the resurrection and the life. He is the light of world, and sends us to be light. But we cannot be the light and salt that Jesus asks us to be if we do not make drastic and definitive lifestyle decisions. It's not about perfection, it's about decisions.

> **WE CANNOT BE THE LIGHT AND SALT THAT JESUS ASKS US TO BE IF WE DO NOT MAKE DRASTIC AND DEFINITIVE LIFESTYLE DECISIONS.**

And that is where these verses become relevant. Most people choose the wide road or the wide gate because it is more comfortable to live like that. For them it is not necessary to make a lot of effort, but only to fulfill some general obligations that calm their conscience before God. They make slight changes in their behavior, but their thinking has not changed.

A true disciple, on the other hand, decides to enter through the narrow gate. They don't care how difficult it is to get through, they choose the narrow road, even though they know it will come with a price. A disciple is one who knows what society offers them and decides to give it up to go after Christ. The narrow path is the path of the disciple and there is great joy there, although the tragedy is that so few people find this path.

🔒 DENY YOURSELF

This is the time for personal questions which can be in a group or individually, depending on how you manage your meetings.

- What are those things that are part of the culture that have seeped into your life?

- What things that go against Scripture are hard for you to let go of?

- How willing or committed are you in your heart to following Christ no matter the consequences?

READ WITH THEM THE FOLLOWING VERSES

Then he said to them all: "Whoever wants to be my disciple must deny themselves and take up their cross daily and follow me. For whoever wants to save their life will lose it, but whoever loses their life for me will save it. What good is it for someone to gain the whole world, and yet lose or forfeit their very self?
Luke 9:23-25

Once we have made an evaluation of our life, it is necessary to deny ourselves, and that means dying to everything that does not please the Lord, even if it is part of the culture and everyone sees it as normal. This is a good time for the discipler along with their disciple to confess to each other their weaknesses and battles. By doing this, both open their hearts and become vulnerable, imperfect, but redeemed by Christ. In this part of the process, the disciple learns to depend on the Holy Spirit for guidance, and the discipler is trained to manifest God's grace to the one they are molding.

Something else to learn:

- The Bible recommends confessing our sins to one another (James 5:16).

- It is good to make a confidentiality agreement that includes both parties.

- Neither is in the position to judge the other (Matthew 7:3).

- Both the mentor and the disciple are being formed by God. There are no steps or hierarchies before the Father; only children giving each other a hand (Galatians 6:2-4).

✋ EMULATE THE CALL

Taking on a challenge involves more than just wishing for the best. It has to do with developing a plan that contains concrete steps to move forward, emulating the call that Christ has given us in sharing on this topic.

SUGGESTED STEPS

The disciple can give thanks for the grace of God by continuing on the narrow road and then pray for a friend who they feel is getting lost in the culture of the world.

The disciple can propose to have a meaningful conversation with a person to stimulate them to live the countercultural gospel of Jesus. (It could be someone to evangelize, or also a Christian who has strayed from the Lord.) And it is important that a date be set. The fact that there is a date will push them to make it happen and to be able to report their result.

While the disciples get used to having these types of conversations with their friends or family, the discipler can accompany and guide them at every step.

It must be clear that we are not the ones who change hearts; that is the role of the Holy Spirit.

LESSON 2

INVASION OF IDEOLOGIES

The problem in our culture is that we are tempted to rely on our own power. So, the challenge for us is to live in such a way that we are radically dependent on and desperate for the power that only God can provide.

David Platt, *Radical*

Imagination and creativity are precious qualities given by God to the human being. They are in our essence. But as is the case with all the good that God has done, because of sin and evil, when things don't have a holy purpose, the imagination and creativity can become toxic.

We live in an age full of philosophies that run like overflowing rivers through the streets and the minds of all. With a communications system that does not filter the positive or the negative and does not even distinguish what is real from what is fictitious, and with public institutions that hide too much information about the reasons for their actions.

To deal with all this, more than good arguments are needed, since the discussion becomes useless in the face of someone who remains stubbornly fixed in their beliefs. It takes clarity and wit.

THE GREAT QUESTION OF THIS SECOND LESSON IS:

How does the gospel differ from all the ideologies that try to seduce young adults today, and what should our reaction to them be?

CHRISTIAN YOUNG ADULTS OF TODAY ASK THEMSELVES:

- "Do non-Christians have valid arguments to believe what they believe?"

- "Why, with their ideologies, are they going against science... or are we the ones who are going against it?"

- "Why is it so difficult to accept the truth of Christ and the logic of morality?"

Masculinity, femininity, and the multiplication of sexual "possibilities" demand from us more analysis and more answers than we have given up to now. Gender identity, for example, has unleashed issues that are being discussed in the legislative arenas of different countries. Thus, for example, abortion has gone from being an attack on life to being a public health alternative, and for these reasons, as children of God it is necessary for us to discuss these matters from a philosophical, scientific, and biblical perspective.

◈ SEE YOUR ENVIRONMENT

Prepare a series of simple, open-ended questions about what today's society believes regarding various specific issues, and let your young adults express themselves by speaking in the third person (i.e., saying what society believes). In the exercise, you may be surprised to learn that many of the young adults in church are advocates of arguments that they are not very knowledgeable on and have no idea they could be wrong. Perhaps because they have found some form of justice in what they promulgate, or because they know someone who thinks this way, or because it seems fair to them to defend the rights of minorities.

To disciple, one needs to be prepared, not only on the solid foundation of God's Word but also to get a responsible reading of what happens in the social circle our disciples are surrounded by. That is why it is good to start with open questions, and not start discussing any mistaken idea that comes to light in this first stage.

Conversing with them about these issues based on questions and not reprimands is an excellent opportunity to find out what is in their hearts and discover what ideas of the world have infiltrated them.

Another possibility, if you want to extend this lesson, is to send your young adults to carry out a survey among their acquaintances, family, friends, and social circles. To do this, prepare a series of straightforward questions that help measure what society believes about these issues. Here are some examples of possible questions:

- What do you think about feminism? Why?

- Why is there such a thing as an LGBTQ+ "movement"?

- What do you think the majority think about abortion and why?

These questions are just examples, and you can create other questions with your group. Most likely there is a talented young adult who would be willing to design a questionnaire for everyone to receive a copy. Make it clear to them that the point of conducting a survey is not to argue with people but to take note of general opinions to later make statistics of the survey carried out. This exercise will be an important contribution to the process, if data can be collected that helps the disciples to measure their environment.

TRAIN TOGETHER

Now is the time to go deeper into the subject and to build a bridge to your personal experiences and opinions. As a discipler, it is obviously in your best interest to be as well prepared as possible, always keeping in mind that these are burning dilemmas in the mind of our young adults. We cannot continue to repeat Christian clichés (even if there is some truth to them).

Find books. Study. The 625.com website has a lot of specific material on hot topics written by health professionals who are mature Christians. Going to science as well as the Bible will add to your authority and conversational skills.

When talking about homosexuality, for example, it is vital that you know that there is no scientific evidence to support the theory that homosexuality is genetically predetermined. This is vital to know, because the mass media have insisted so much on planting this idea within society that many today affirm it as if it were something that cannot be discussed. But it should be discussed and, in fact, according to the most serious scientific studies in the world (in which homosexual scientists have even participated), nothing has ever been certified about a genetic predisposition, which indicates that it is a human decision, surely initially unconscious, but human decision nonetheless.

As children of God, we are called to find the proper foundations to argue wisely and intelligently when we encounter such a lack of reason.

PROPOSAL

- Investigate the studies of Francis Collins, American geneticist, discoverer of the human genome.

- Watch interviews with Roxanna Kreimer, PhD and creator of the "Scientific Feminism-2" Facebook page, which tries to dismiss the weak arguments of radical feminism from a philosophical and scientific position.

- Choose some videos of different political scientists and journalists who are opponents of gender movements and their political interference.

- Find the history of the origins of the LGBTQ+ movement and its main exponents.

- Learn the fundamental human rights and the main universal declarations.

You could distribute these points as homework to different members of your discipleship group or choose one or two points to work on personally.

Disciples must be trained to think and act like Christ. And he always had a timely answer for every aspect of life, not just spiritual things. Jesus spoke about marriage, about the relationship between siblings, about how to value

AS CHILDREN OF GOD, WE ARE CALLED TO FIND THE PROPER FOUNDATIONS TO ARGUE WISELY AND INTELLIGENTLY.

parents and how to treat friends. He spoke about obeying the laws and respecting authorities. His great sermons referred to daily areas of life, such as planting and harvesting, and also to the management of personal and home finances. And, of course, Jesus also had to deal with the social problems of his day, such as promiscuity and adultery.

Jesus's answers were different for each case. We see Jesus deal firmly with those who showed hardness of heart, like some Pharisees, but in cases of promiscuity like the woman caught in adultery, we see that he had great mercy. Perhaps because she showed that she was sorry and willing to receive whatever punishment it was. We do not know. But we see that his words towards her were kind and forgiving, although with great advice behind them: "Go and sin no more."

We, in our daily walk, will meet different types of people as well. Those who seek Jesus with a yearning heart, those who categorically reject him, those who say they oppose and in their interior cry out to meet him, and those whose hearts are so wounded that they aim to offend the principles in which we believe.

The key will always be the same: see people as Jesus sees them.

Having said this, there is something important that we must differentiate: **one battle is fought at the ideological level, and another is fought for the people that Jesus loves, although both have a spiritual component.** Jesus condemned the ideology of the Pharisees and Sadducees, who defended doctrines that were not commanded by God, but he did not set out to exclude these people without choice. He demonstrated this, for example, when he taught Nicodemus, a Pharisee, about the new birth in chapter 3 of the Gospel of John.

ONE BATTLE IS FOUGHT AT THE IDEOLOGICAL LEVEL, AND ANOTHER IS FOUGHT FOR THE PEOPLE.

The battle for souls is the mission for which we are on earth. It is a divine commission to reach those whom the Father seeks, because he wants everyone to be saved and no one to be lost (2 Peter 3:9). That battle has to do with the way we relate to the world, to people. If we walk with a turned-up nose as if we smell sin in everything and everyone, we probably will not be able to get close to the people we want to save... and that would not be the correct attitude of a true disciple.

If we impose the burden of the law and condemnation on those who are lost, we will close more doors than we will open. We must, rather, learn to love them, even if we do not share their ideas and behavior. We must open spaces where they can feel heard and loved, so that they keep the door of their heart open to the gospel. We must talk to them about their needs and tell them about the One who can supply each one of them.

When we feel inclined to point out the sin in each person, it often helps to remember where we were when God rescued us; remember that we too were in a pit full of mud and putrefaction and that Jesus didn't mind going down there to clean us up and take us to his heights. Jesus did it out of compassion for the lost, and so should we.

As you teach and learn to see people in this way, ask your young adults how they were treated when they came to the feet of Christ. It is also good to remember who was there to help them: shoulders on which they cried; friends who, with love and patience, accompanied them on this road to Emmaus; ears that were willing to comfort and not criticize. That is the relational part: gospel, grace, and mercy.

The ideological battle, on the other hand, is at an intellectual level. We need to have a position against the proposals of the current world. For that we cannot use what we hear on the streets or see on television, nor have criteria based on bad personal experiences or value judgments, nor opt for a religious position that instead of looking for rational answers only works as a wall that does not allow people to approach to ask questions.

WHEN WE FEEL INCLINED TO POINT OUT THE SIN IN EACH PERSON, IT OFTEN HELPS TO REMEMBER WHERE WE WERE WHEN GOD RESCUED US.

It is necessary first to have listened carefully to others and their interests: what are their ideals and what are they fighting for? Then we must assess whether their motives make any sense. Usually, most of the people who are in favor of these movements have no idea what they are asking for. It only seems to them that they defend "a good cause" and want to ingratiate themselves with these groups because, in their opinion, "it is unfair that they deny their requests." They therefore have an unfounded solidarity.

Because of this, we must generate arguments based on sociology, logic, biology, and the search for the integral well-being of society in order to help these people to reflect on their own arguments. At the same time, we must learn to recognize the political influence behind the various movements that, although subtle, does exist.

Remember: **we fight two battles. The battle for souls** makes us seek and love those whom God loves, without distinction, and **the ideological battle** makes us raise our voices to denounce what is wrong in society and defend correct values.

RUMINATE ON A MODEL

BEN SHAPIRO

Ben Shapiro is a loved or hated lawyer who graduated summa cum laude from Harvard University who works as a writer, journalist, and political commentator. He is of Jewish background and, together with his wife, practices Orthodox Judaism.

It would be impossible to say that he is right in each of his arguments in all the topics he normally discusses but even if we disagree with him on many of them, we have to agree that Shapiro is notable for how he contrasts some of the popular ideas disseminated in the media. He has become an example of someone who knows how to argue with logical, sociological, philosophical, and scientific arguments, also generally keeping his cool.

📖 ILLUMINATE YOURSELF WITH THE TRUTH

Sexual immorality existed from the earliest times described in the Bible. Genesis tells the story of Sodom and Gomorrah, two cities given over to sexual sin, and describes acts of rape (2 Samuel 13), incest (Genesis 19:36), homosexuality (Genesis 19:5), and adultery (2 Samuel 11:4-5).

We must understand that, although they have different consequences, all sins of a sexual nature come from the same root, which is sexual immorality. One is not worse than the other, so both homosexuality and bisexuality and all the trends that have emerged in recent times are similar to other behaviors of this nature such as pornography, adultery, fornication, etc.

The New Testament uses the Greek word *porneia* to define all forms of sexual immorality, and from there all wrong behaviors related to sexuality are derived.

Chapter 1 of the book of Romans describes a process or set of conditions that trigger sexual immorality in people. We recommend you read the entire chapter to be able to analyze it little by little. Verses 18 through 20 talk about the manifestation of God through all visible things, and contrast this with the refusal of human beings who, despite seeing God in all things, decide to turn their backs on him. Verse 21 is forceful:

> *For although they knew God, they neither glorified him as God nor gave thanks to him, but their thinking became futile and their foolish hearts were darkened. Although they claimed to be wise, they became fools.*
> **Romans 1:21–22**

The consequence of this foolishness led human beings to idolatry, as described in verse 23 and, finally, to a tendency to corrupt his sexuality through the cult of the satisfaction of bodily desires, as it says in verse 24. Verse 25 tells about what has always happened in the ideological sphere, from Genesis, to the time of Jesus, in the time of the apostles, and even now:

> *They exchanged the truth about God for a lie, and worshiped and served created things rather than the Creator—who is forever praised. Amen.*
> **Romans 1:25**

Here we read how people turned their backs on God's truth to believe the lie expounded by the ideologies of this world. Then, from verse 26 onward, there is talk of all kinds of perversions, sexual immorality, and all kinds of behaviors that, although they are related to each other, end up affecting different areas of the human being.

If you explore the text well, you will realize that the origin of everything is the foolishness of people for not listening to God's truth. From this perspective, the only way for a person to change their way of thinking and acting is that they receive the revelation of Christ in their life and their eyes will be opened so that they decide to get closer to God. This will not happen by human efforts, since we are not the ones who convince anyone of sin, but that is the role of the Holy Spirit (John 16:8).

The revolution that belongs to you as a disciple from now on is not found in the proclamation of the truths of Romans 1, but in the conclusive verse 1 of Romans 2, which many seem to forget to read:

> *You, therefore, have no excuse, you who pass judgment on someone else,*
> *for at whatever point you judge another, you are condemning yourself,*
> *because you who pass judgment do the same things.*
> **Romans 2:1**

Wow! Did you read that? You are probably telling yourself that you are not like them, but Scripture says that you are! Consider, for example, that when Jesus spoke of adultery, he mentioned not only the act but also the thought, desire, and intentions of the heart... and we are not exempt from that. All human beings have a powerful tendency toward sin. For this reason, we are not in a position to be able to judge anyone, especially when we recognize that we would be taking that right away from the one and only sovereign God. On the contrary, we are called to love all people in all circumstances.

This is probably why Paul, the writer of the letter to the Romans, placed special emphasis throughout the following chapters on making us understand that no one saves themself, no one is free from sin (Romans 3:23), no one is in a position to judge others (Romans 2:3), and, above all, that each person on earth has the urgent need to know Christ, since due to the sin that lives in each one of us (Romans 7:21) we all need to be saved by his redeeming grace (Romans 4:25).

It would really be worth it for you and those you are discipling to carefully read through the entire book of Romans!

Of course, the fact that we see all people with love does not mean that we can't maintain a firm position in favor of holiness, sexual purity, an education free of ideologies, and that we fight so that our biblical conviction is heard and respected. Although we cannot force anyone to listen to it, nor should we impose it on them, we must raise our voice so that it is heard and received by those hearts that the Lord in his mercy wants to touch, and so that the entire society knows that we are there; not asleep or silent as if we were slaves, but rather on the warpath. A war of love for the world that God loves (John 3:16-17).

🔒 DENY YOURSELF

It is very likely that your young adults feel overwhelmed by so much ideological confusion. After doing enough research, including giving them enough biblical, philosophical, and scientific bases so that they have a personal opinion about it, it is time for each person to reflect on themselves. Consider having a time of prayer, together or separately, where you as a discipler intercede for them so that they receive God's truth and develop firm convictions in their faith.

You can practice the following exercise with your youth. Tell them the following:

Let's imagine that we had been around the woman who was caught in adultery. We have two stones, one in each hand, and we are ready to enforce the law that says that woman should be stoned to death. Suddenly, we hear the words of Jesus saying: "He who is without sin, cast the first stone," and these words make us realize that we are in a position in which we should not be. We feel Jesus's gaze upon us. Surely, we would end up throwing the two stones on the ground. Now, what would those two stones that we had to drop mean?

This exercise has to do with removing from our lives certain attitudes that make us sinners before God and, consequently, subject to his judgment.

Some examples of what these stones could represent are:

- Judgments: I have been one of those who judge without thinking about the people God loves.

- Criticism: I have been one of those who speak without having an adequate foundation, just to spread a rumor or discredit another.

- Sexual immorality: I have succumbed to sins of a sexual nature; pornography, adultery, fornication, lust, lasciviousness, or sinful thoughts and desires.

- Lack of mercy: I have had the opportunity to help someone who is struggling with some type of sexual immorality, and I have denied them that help.

- Irresponsibility: I have preferred to stay away from this type of conversation so as not to lose friends, or so that they do not know about my faith and my convictions.

Help your young adults to search deep in their hearts and to give up any stone that prevents them from being more like Jesus.

This is a good time to confess to any struggle in this area. If one of your young adults has had, for example, a sinful desire, it is time to confess it, not to make it a moment of shame but to unleash a new freedom.

As a discipler, you must be prepared for this. In some cases, you may need to refer one of your youth to a therapist or psychological professional who supports your ministry and practices the Christian faith. Ministries such as "Free in Christ" or similar ones, which offer help on these types of issues, can also be useful.

EMULATE THE CALL

To define the next steps, these questions are useful:

- How can I defend my faith in front of a person who openly defends gender identity?

- How can I represent Jesus faithfully when I disagree with people?

Just as this lesson began with a discussion to present opinions, close the lesson in the same way, but now asking open-ended questions about what they have learned and better understand about what the Bible says. It might even be good for some of them to speak on these issues with the teens, as this will serve the teen ministry and affirm the findings and convictions in your teens as well. That young adults can be a positive influence for adolescents is one of the goals of Generational Leadership, and it is also a great launching pad for those you are discipling to move toward their own maturity.

LESSON 3

THE CHALLENGE OF CHARACTER

True transformation happens little by little. With small changes that end up becoming collective habits. It begins with small seeds that, with patience and time, immerse a field, in more humble but lasting ways. It may not be spectacular, but it's real.

Alex Sampedro, *Craftsman*

Being more like Jesus each day should be about our internal values; our way of being, thinking, and then, acting. In other words, it's more about character than behaviors.

Character flaws that are not overcome while we are young will be a stumbling block to our healing and performance in adulthood.

Someone immature, even an adult, can destroy their most important relationships, squander career opportunities, and faint when they most need to be on their feet. Due to immaturity, loved ones are hurt. Marriages and families are destroyed by immaturity. Because of immaturity, envy or greed can be harbored in the heart. And due to immaturity, many can fall into addictions from which it will be difficult for them to get out.

⬡ SEE YOUR ENVIRONMENT

Ask your young adults to complete the following survey. In this list of "character defects," each one should choose a number from 1 to 5 to represent their personal situation (1 if it is something that does not control them at all; 5 if they recognize that it is a major defect in their life). In this way they will be able to evaluate which are the most urgent aspects on which they must work.

Envy _____	Authoritarianism _____	Starting things I don't end up finishing _____
Desires of Revenge _____	Irritability _____	Not recognizing my own mistakes _____
Selfishness _____	Laziness _____	Arrogance _____
Pride _____	Jealousy _____	Tendency to lie _____
Vanity _____	Apathy _____	Self-justification _____
Resentment _____	Aggression _____	Emotional instability _____
Intransigence _____	Being in a bad mood _____	Constant criticism _____
Irrational fears _____	Possessiveness _____	Dependency on others _____

Sometimes it's hard to be objective when evaluating ourselves, right? A second option is that you can send your young adults this list of "character defects" and ask them to find some people close to them who know them well and ask them to fill out the same survey. Parents and siblings may be good candidates, but it will also work with your closest friends. Even you, as a discipler, could make an evaluation of each one of your disciples, although it is necessary that you emphasize that the important thing is not to just put a score but to evaluate in order to help and love better.

At the end of this process, they will collect the data and compare it. It may come as a surprise for many to observe the differences between their own evaluation and those of others. And it will be very interesting for each one to know the

YOUR VULNERABILITIES CAN BE THE BEST PULPIT FOR YOUR INFLUENCE.

way others see them, especially if they are people they live with or are close to (although you may want to consider making the surveys anonymous so that no one can feel hurt by a particular person's comments).

TRAIN TOGETHER

On the outside we can fake many things, but it is what's in the heart that reflects our true being, and the more we let God mold our character, the greater the positive influence we can have in the world. Then we will be a better tool in the hands of God to fulfill his purpose.

This is the moment to land an honest personal testimony, remembering that your vulnerabilities can be the best pulpit for your influence.

In this sense, one of the things that all disciples must be clear about is that times of trial and difficulty will come so that our character can be formed. Each test passed will be one more step toward our own maturity and potentially that of others.

Failing a test means that the test will return.

There are several necessary foundations for the construction of character. Pastor Héctor Plaza, in his book, *El carácter del líder (The Character of the Leader)* mentions five: the Word of God as the fundamental basis of every child of God; the integrity that makes us people of our word; the obedience that makes us trustworthy; the willingness to be teachable that gives us the ability to constantly learn; and the ease to be humble that makes us recognize when we are wrong and helps us to start again.

These five aspects are essential foundations which are formed as we make decisions, some of them difficult; little by little they bring a weight of maturity to those who have been trained in it. What, then, are the things that lay the groundwork for building a strong character?

- **A life of constant communication with God**. While it's true that we all have different ways of connecting with God, we need to make that connection regularly.

- **Spiritual disciplines.** Worship, prayer, fasting, reading and studying the Word of God, meditation and memorization of his Word are all good disciplines that a disciple must develop to form a strong character.

- **Accountability.** Having someone to whom we can voluntarily give an account of our life promotes a strength in our inner being that is difficult to replicate. When we are vulnerable to someone else, we become people of increasingly strong character. This also makes us humbler and prevents us from stumbling.

- **Firm convictions.** The fact of not letting ourselves be blown away by the winds of information means that we are not like the waves of the sea, as the letter of James says.

- **Appropriate management of emotions.** Emotional reactions arise from an immature character and need to be controlled. It is not that emotions are wrong, just that our actions or decisions should not be based on emotions, but on a balance of soul and spirit.

- **Self-control.** Emotional reactions arise from an immature character and need to be controlled. We cannot be controlled by our emotions.

RUMINATE ON A MODEL

JOYCE MEYER

Perhaps you have heard of Joyce Meyer. This Christian writer and speaker, born in 1943 in St. Louis, Missouri, United States, deals with many character issues in her lectures and books, and always exposes her own healing processes.

As with all the people we consider in this book, she is not someone perfect, and we could not say that we agree with everything she has said or written. Yet her testimony is very gripping, since her father sexually abused her on a weekly basis for years in addition to having an angry and intimidating relationship with her. Growing up with this weight on her shoulders, at a certain point Joyce decided to talk to her mother, but she did not believe her, as happens with many mothers or fathers who receive a complaint of this nature. In her book *Beauty from Ashes*, Joyce recounts how, on one occasion, when she was fourteen, her mother came home to find her husband sexually abusing Joyce; her reaction was to get out of there and come back two hours later as if nothing had happened.

Her father's abuse and her mother's betrayal made her decide to run away from home at the age of eighteen to marry the first man she found. Unsurprisingly, the man was a manipulator, thief, and con man. Joyce says that she was about to go crazy when she was barely twenty-one years old, and had a miscarriage followed by the birth of her first child. Also, as if that wasn't enough, her husband had abandoned her to go live with another woman two blocks from her own house, claiming that the child Joyce was carrying was not his.

To recount all the sad stories and critical moments in Joyce's life would be to delve into a pool of disasters that brought her devastation, fear of everything, and relational and emotional incapacity to face life. But God had great things for her, as well as for all of us who decide to believe in him. Joyce had to learn to trust people, God, and herself again. She had to learn to get up despite feeling exhausted from having fallen so many times, she had to overcome her fears and discard her old habits to change them for new ones, and she had to tear out her disturbed mind to put on the mind of Christ and thus completely renew her life. If you look at Joyce now, you will see a confident woman, someone who not only preaches and teaches with authority, but lives with the strength of character she has developed. And this does not mean that she has become hard-hearted, but that, in the sensitivity of her heart, she has known how to overcome the attacks of life and has learned to believe God.

It does not matter how many misfortunes we have experienced, how much of a disadvantage we believe we are in, how many mistakes we have made, or the barriers that we face that do not let us move forward. The only thing that matters is that we have a God who can make all things new and who uses everything that happens to us to shape our character to be similar to the character of Jesus. That is the challenge of discipleship. Look more like him.

📖 ILLUMINATE YOURSELF WITH THE TRUTH

As you come to him, the living Stone—rejected by humans but chosen by God and precious to him—you also, like living stones, are being built into a spiritual house to be a holy priesthood, offering spiritual sacrifices acceptable to God through Jesus Christ.

1 Peter 2:4–5

Here the apostle Peter tells us about Christ as the living stone, a foundation on which we build our lives. The material of this foundation is heavenly, eternal, and precious. It refers to the attributes and character of Christ. In the same way, Peter speaks to the church, and consequently to each one of us, assuring us that we are living stones just like Jesus, since the Father builds us with the same heavenly, eternal, and precious material as Christ. This speaks of what we are in essence: a spiritual house!

Also, a stone is part of an altar. Therefore, we are also the lit altar of living stones on which sacrifices of worship to the Father are performed. As long as the foundation is laid in Jesus, the living stone, the eternal rock, we will be building this spiritual house well.

Our condition and growth are so important in the construction process of the church that if a stone does not fulfill its proper function, the entire building is at risk. Christ is the example, and for this reason he is the foundation. In him there is no deceit or shadow of doubt. Jesus fulfilled all the law and was perfect in everything.

> *To this you were called, because Christ suffered for you, leaving you an example, that you should follow in his steps. "He committed no sin, and no deceit was found in his mouth." When they hurled their insults at him, he did not retaliate; when he suffered, he made no threats. Instead, he entrusted himself to him who judges justly. "He himself bore our sins" in his body on the cross, so that we might die to sins and live for righteousness; "by his wounds you have been healed."*
> **1 Peter 2:21–24**

Following in the footsteps of Christ means turning your back on sin. To be molded according to the character of Christ is to cross the desert of doubt and not stop believing; suffer judgment and shame and respond meekly; suffer injustice and act with self-control; to be rejected, hurt, and betrayed, yet despite all this have a forgiving spirit. All these actions define a mature character.

QUESTIONS TO REFLECT ON

- How do you respond when you are insulted?

- What is your reaction when an injustice is committed against you?

- What do you do when someone lies to you?

- How do you act when someone makes you suffer?

- What feelings do you have against the people who have hurt you?

IDEALLY, WE WOULD BE SO ALIGNED WITH THE VOICE OF THE SPIRIT OF GOD THAT EVERY REACTION WE HAVE IS CONTROLLED BY HIM.

Each of these questions can help us to assess our degree of maturity. It's not just about putting your head down and letting the whole world run over you. On the contrary, ideally, we would be so aligned with the voice of the Spirit of God that every response we have is controlled by him. Even strong reactions and complaints can be mature actions, rather than temper tantrums. There are stages of development in the physical world, from childhood to adulthood. In the same way, there are stages from immaturity to maturity as children of God.

When the heart of a child of God is governed by Christ, their desires will be satisfied, and that will make sinful desires dissipate, because what brings satisfaction to their life is Christ. But if their heart has areas that are not governed by Jesus, these areas will be immature and will be carried away by the desires of the flesh.

How can we realize that there is an area of our being that is not filled by Christ? The answer to this question is obtained by identifying the temptations that we recurrently give in to. The child of God who has allowed themselves to be molded and filled by Christ will be someone who will act more like him. Thus, they will become mature children.

It is interesting to note that the New Testament uses three words that are translated as "child" and whose meanings are related to maturity:

1. *TEKNION*

   ◊ It refers to the child who is small, who cannot fend for themselves and therefore depends on someone else. The Bible says that these children still need guardians because, although they are heirs, they cannot make their inheritance effective due to their immaturity. At this stage the word *nepios* is also used to refer to a small and immature child.

◊ In John 13:33 Jesus uses the word *teknion* for his disciples, making them see that they were just newborns, but they were not yet ready.

◊ In 1 John 2:1 the writer also uses the word *teknion* to refer to those of his disciples who still struggled with the same sins, not to judge them, but to remind them that Christ has forgiven their sins, even though they are not yet able to avoid them.

2. *TEKNON*

◊ This refers to a child who has already gone through some processes and has taken growth steps. They have demonstrated, based on their decisions and lifestyle, not only that they follow Christ but that they have been willing to be formed by him.

◊ In Galatians 4:19 Paul uses the word *teknon* to refer to those spiritual children who had developed to such an extent that their maturing process is likened by Paul as labor pains, alluding to the suffering caused by the formation of a spiritual child, that is, of a disciple. However, the *teknon* is not yet sufficiently mature.

◊ In Romans 9:8-11 Paul uses the word *teknon* to refer to those spiritual children who are maturing with respect to their purpose and are heading toward their calling.

3. *HUIOS*

◊ This is the type of child who has matured enough to take responsibility, having responded positively to their formation processes. They are a child who has acquired the mature criteria of the Father.

◊ In Luke 9:35, the voice of the Father that comes from heaven affirms the maturity of Jesus, the Son in whom he is pleased. There the term *huios* is used.

◊ At the beginning of the Gospel of Matthew, the same term is also used to refer to Jesus.

DISCIPLES ARE IN CONSTANT GROWTH TOWARD FORMATION AS MATURE CHILDREN.

Disciples are in constant growth toward formation as mature children. A disciple is essentially a maturing child of God, someone who passes through the growth processes in which they are tested. Early on they receive simple tasks and sometimes fail to obey, but, as time goes by, they take steps of greater obedience and blossom into mature disciples.

An immature child cannot receive greater responsibilities from the Father. He still asks for food and shelter, and begs for protection, instead of confidently knowing that the Father will always provide, protect, and supply what is necessary, just as a mature child would think.

DENY YOURSELF

In a world in which people are urged to let themselves be guided by what they want in the moment, it is urgent to identify what is necessary and important, to separate it from what is only filler. Pride usually resembles a balloon inflated with a lot of useless air, which over time ends up escaping. A proud disciple has not learned to be like Jesus in that area. This is someone who thinks that they do not make mistakes, who justifies themselves for everything, and who does not accept advice but lives in the foolishness of their heart. If there is any poison that contaminates a person's soul, it is pride. And, like all poison, one must identify it and uproot it from one's life.

Some forms of pride are:

- **Familial pride**, by surname or lineage. This type of pride makes us feel more valuable or important than others because we were born in a certain family.

- **Racial pride**. Many times, we are motivated to feel proud of our race or social condition, but Scripture says that the Father does not make a distinction between Jews or Greeks, nor does he pay attention to nationalities or races, but he looks at hearts.

> IN A WORLD IN WHICH PEOPLE ARE URGED TO LET THEMSELVES BE GUIDED BY WHAT THEY WANT IN THE MOMENT, IT IS URGENT TO IDENTIFY WHAT IS NECESSARY AND IMPORTANT.

- **Being hard-hearted**. When a person's heart has been hardened, it does not allow the Word of God enter; as a result, that person cannot be molded into the image of Christ.

- **Arrogance.** This form of pride includes trying to show off, being noticed, or wanting others to recognize you as better than others.

- **Haughtiness**. Scripture mentions haughty eyes and heart, and this speaks of the condition of our inner being. Someone haughty may not be proud in front of others, but internally they feel they are superior.

Denying yourself in the area of pride could mean giving in to an argument despite knowing you are right, or learning to admit a mistake, or reaching out to apologize when necessary.

✋ EMULATE THE CALL

A useful exercise and a good long-term commitment for disciples is to evaluate ourselves periodically to keep any character vices at bay.

A wake-up call can be identifying these phrases in our own lives:

1. Self-sufficient pride:

    ◊   I do not need anybody.

    ◊   I can do it alone.

    ◊   I don't like asking for help.

2. Pride of scorn:

    ◊   I feel that I am more valuable than others.

    ◊   I value people for what they do and not for who they are.

    ◊   I can't see good things in others.

3. Pride of unforgiveness:

    ◊   I cannot forgive one or more people.

    ◊   I resent others easily.

    ◊   I lose control easily and flare up in anger.

4. Pride of reputation:

    ◊   I feel that I don't deserve anyone's love or attention.

    ◊   I say I don't care if I was hurt or abandoned.

    ◊   I don't like to express my emotions.

5. Pride of stubbornness:

    ◊   I can't admit that I was wrong.

    ◊   I don't accept suggestions from others easily.

    ◊   It annoys or hurts me if my idea is not carried out to a T.

6. Hard-hearted pride:

    ◊   I cannot accept biblical truths easily.

    ◊   I don't hurt for the circumstances of others.

    ◊   I am selfish and greedy.

    ◊   I do not take God into account when managing money.

    ◊   The idea of giving to God's work bothers me.

    ◊   I give excuses for not giving tithes and offerings.

7. Pride of rebellion:

    ◊   I find it difficult to submit to authorities.

    ◊   I like to argue, creating an atmosphere of conflict.

    ◊   I encourage others to rebel or fight.

8. Pride of exaltation:

    ◊   I come across as arrogant at times.

    ◊   I continually brag about things I've done.

    ◊   I like others to recognize me and congratulate me for my work.

    ◊   I like to be first in everything, and it annoys me when I'm not.

    ◊   I can't stand others being recognized, admired, or praised.

◊ It is difficult for me to work in a team or to give up my place or position.

Noticing the presence of these attitudes, it is good to make a personal plan to change those habits related to pride and what is behind them. The call is to continue growing in emulating Jesus, and in this we will be able to advance in maturity.

LESSON 4

REASON AND FAITH

Demonizing intelligence and critical thinking are giving the enemy tools that do not belong to him.

Alex Sampedro, *Craftsman*

Science and faith are not enemies. On the contrary, they are powerful when they join forces for human benefit. There are challenges that science will never overcome without faith, and faith will never be enough when science is needed.

Reason and faith must go hand in hand. This topic is essential for young adults because it is at universities where it becomes more noticeable that many thinkers have turned away from the faith, and an enormous number of believers have renounced science. Arguments come and go to justify each side's statements without thinking about the possibility that they could walk together.

> **MANY THINKERS HAVE TURNED AWAY FROM FAITH, AND AN ENORMOUS NUMBER OF BELIEVERS HAVE RENOUNCED SCIENCE.**

Divorcing faith from reason is unjustified because both tools are necessary and compatible for integral human maturation.

◈ SEE YOUR ENVIRONMENT

Send your youth to review some of the arguments for atheism. You can compare statistical data of atheists in your country. This exercise will allow them to have an approach to a world that believers usually do not want to see. You will notice that, in addition to atheism, they will come across other perspectives that it would also be good for them to know about, such as deism, theism, and others.

They can even analyze their family environment. From an extended family structure, considering parents, uncles, grandparents, first and second cousins, and all relatives, they can conduct interviews to find out:

- How many consider themselves believers?

- How many consider themselves spiritual, but not religious?

- Which of them considers that faith is more significant than what science says?

- Who among them considers that science has arguments that faith cannot explain?

- Are there any deists or theists among them? (We'll explain more about this later.)

- Do any of them consider themselves Gnostic or Agnostic?

- How many of them are part of a religion other than Christianity?

Analyzing their families based on these questions will help the young adult have a clearer picture of their family's beliefs. As you will see, there are more than just "believers" and "nonbelievers." There is a very complex range of attitudes and reactions regarding the gospel. Having this analysis of your family's beliefs in writing can provide interesting guidelines for each young adult.

🚆 TRAIN TOGETHER

The behavior of human beings is governed by what they believe and think. If there is a recurring behavior, whatever it may be, it will always be linked to the person's thoughts. From the simplest things, like crossing the street or deciding what to wear, to the most extreme behaviors, like addictions and obsessive behaviors, all are the consequence of what the mind believes.

If our actions are determined by what we think, then Paul was right when he said we must renew our minds. He was not referring only to the moment of conversion to Christ. In fact, converting to Jesus is not simply about an intellectual act (in the sense of having believed something and, from that point, beginning to have faith in the Savior), but rather, it is a gradual process of small encounters that go deeper into the mind and heart of the person until at the end, they surrender in faith. This is the work of the Holy Spirit.

EVERYTHING WE DO IS LINKED TO WHAT WE THINK.

It is true that everything we do is linked to what we think; from this point of view, thought describes what we believe in. Without thought, faith would never have existed, although today, many of us who believe in Christ tend to ignore the value of accurate and critical thinking. This happens, perhaps, because we were taught not to debate the things of God and what the Scriptures say but to accept them without question. This is a mistake, and there are testimonies from great thinkers who were initially atheists and who, determined to prove the nonexistence of God, ended up finding God. This happened because they decided to question themselves about it. Of course, we are not talking about arrogant and challenging questioning but about asking honest questions.

FOR EXAMPLE

Someone tells you that they believe in evolution. You, as a Christian, tell them that you believe that God made everything Then they mock you because they tell you that the theory of evolution is proven, which is practically impossible, hence it is named a theory. This theory is a possible explanation of how the progression of the species occurred, yet it still has some notable loose links.

THINK FOR A MOMENT

Is it verifiable that in the history of creation there were species that have adapted better to certain circumstances than others?

The answer is yes.

However...

How does that deny that God started the process?

The practical reality is that many people think the exact same thing, but some will tell you that they believe in the theory of evolution and others will tell you that they believe in the theory of creationism.

The wise thing is to ask the right questions, and Christians must be humble enough to recognize that we do not have the answers to all the questions related to creation, precisely because God wants us to develop reason and science to discover our own answers.

RUMINATE ON A MODEL

WILLIAM LANE CRAIG

William Lane Craig is a philosopher and theologian recognized as one of the greatest expositors in the defense of the gospel throughout the world.

In a society where many people doubt the existence of God, we need more men like this, who will rise up to say the opposite as a prophetic and scientific voice.

One of his most famous defenses has to do with the origin of the universe. The Kalam cosmological argument, which consists of three statements, goes like this:

1. Everything that begins to exist has a cause for its existence.

2. The universe began to exist.

3. The universe has a cause for its existence.

Using this principle, Craig defends that which is the first cause without a cause: God. One of his most famous books, which inspired us to write this chapter, is entitled *Reasonable Faith*. If we could recommend a single book that talks about uniting reason and faith, this would be it!

People like William Lane Craig are examples to us that we do not need to abandon our faith the moment we feel our arguments are weak, but we must investigate and learn so as to fashion our arguments in such a way that the world (which screams that God does not exist) can respect and listen to our investigation.

Since we cannot persuade everyone, our goal should be to make our cumulative apologetic case as persuasive as possible. This can best be done by appealing to facts that are widely accepted or to intuitions that are commonly shared (common sense).
William Lane Craig *(Reasonable Faith)*

A true disciple of Jesus will be filled with the best arguments to defend their faith. This is how Craig has done it, and this is how we can do it.

📖 ILLUMINATE YOURSELF WITH THE TRUTH

For many, the Bible is a book of faith and spiritual matters. However, the Word of God contains much more than just arguments of faith. In it you will find detailed history, philosophy, and science, although it is not scientific in nature nor is that its purpose.

As the author of Hebrews says:

> *For the word of God is alive and active. Sharper than any double-edged sword, it penetrates even to dividing soul and spirit, joints and marrow; it judges the thoughts and attitudes of the heart. Nothing in all creation is hidden from God's sight. Everything is uncovered and laid bare before the eyes of him to whom we must give account.*
> **Hebrews 4:12–13**

This text speaks of the blunt power of the Word of God. But where is such power evidenced, so that we can be sure that it is real? Certainly in its ability to touch the very depth of the two fundamental aspects inherent to human beings: our thoughts and the intentions of our heart.

On the one hand, there is what is in the mind, and on the other, what the heart says. On one side are the arguments, and on the other, the emotions. On one side is knowledge, and on the other, conviction. The Word of God helps us to reconcile both realities.

For the concepts we have believed before understanding them, a deep study of the Word of God helps us to better understand them. For the concepts that we have understood with our minds without being able to fully believe them, the Word of God helps us to experience them, thus taking us to new levels of faith.

In verse 13 above we are told that everything has been created by him, and therefore nothing is hidden from him. God, who knows the heart of each person, knows that some reject the gospel because of intellectual disputes and some because of wounds to the soul, yet both can be softened through the power of his Word.

Now meditate on this other passage of Scripture:

> *Jesus replied: "'Love the Lord your God with all your heart and with all your soul and with all your mind.' This is the first and greatest commandment. And the second is like it: 'Love your neighbor as yourself'."*
> **Matthew 22:37-39**

When Jesus was asked what the most important commandment was, he answered this: love God with your heart, soul, and mind. When he talks about the mind, he refers to an intellectual faith. By this, we know that we do not have a blind faith, but a faith that is filled with the knowledge of his Word to sustain the foundation of this faith. If we only stayed with what the heart believes or what the soul feels, then our way of loving God would be incomplete; we can't be divided. Our mind must be satisfied, just like our emotions, through personal encounters with the Creator.

OUR MIND MUST BE SATISFIED, JUST LIKE OUR EMOTIONS, THROUGH PERSONAL ENCOUNTERS WITH THE CREATOR.

Sometimes we are led to believe that argumentation is negative for our faith, but it is not. On the contrary, having better arguments strengthens our faith to such an extent that it is invincible.

In his book *Evidence That Demands a Verdict,* Josh McDowell quotes John Warmick and Herbert Butterfield, who argue that you cannot separate the Jesus of history from the Jesus of faith. This means that our faith is genuine as long as it remains faithful to the historical reality of the existence of Jesus, his words, and his deeds. For this reason, both the faith of spiritual conviction and structurally thought faith are areas that complement each other.

For we did not follow cleverly devised stories when we told you about the coming of our Lord Jesus Christ in power, but we were eyewitnesses of his majesty.
2 Peter 1:16

In this verse the apostle Peter confronts the thoughts of many of those present regarding the veracity of his preaching. It was not about fairy tales or invented things, and for this reason the best argument that Peter had was to tell them: "I was there, I saw it with my own eyes, I touched it, I lived it, I experienced it with my heart!" Since that time, the veracity of everything that happened with Jesus and what the Word of God recounts is validated based on the testimony of many. And there is so much truth there that knowing it brings us freedom!

We also have the prophetic message as something completely reliable, and you will do well to pay attention to it, as to a light shining in a dark place, until the day dawns and the morning star rises in your hearts.
2 Peter 1:19

What Peter says is true. The fulfillment of the prophecies is an analysis of indisputable facts, and we will do well to examine them carefully, because each one gives us certainty of the truth that is in them. Here we see once again how the careful examination of Scriptures can lead us to a firm conviction, which will be like a torch in the places of greatest darkness, that is, the places of least faith.

🔒 DENY YOURSELF

We cannot deny our doubts because it is natural and even positive to have them.

Why? Because through them we learn. When we have doubts about something it is because we want to know about that something. We feel intrigued and curious, and that is a mechanism designed by God for our learning. What we must refuse is to ignore or hide our doubts.

As disciples of Christ, we must work on our doubts to develop an increasingly solid faith. A doubt that we leave unresolved, either for fear of facing it or because we are lazy, can become a virus capable of contaminating even the depths of our mind. When doubt, which is good, is used by Satan, who is bad, he will try to use it to affect your faith, since he will go for what you are not sure of.

It is not possible to be in the middle, serve two masters, believe half of the things, or have a different faith according to the occasion. Deny yourself the desire to do nothing with your doubts. Anyone who becomes a disciple must decide to renounce all forms of doctrine that go against their faith, they must not do so blindly, but proactively investigate and develop sound arguments to defend what they believe.

A DOUBT THAT WE LEAVE UNRESOLVED, EITHER FOR FEAR OF FACING IT OR BECAUSE WE ARE LAZY, CAN BECOME A VIRUS CAPABLE OF CONTAMINATING OUR MIND.

EMULATE THE CALL

Encourage your young adults to discuss faith with non-Christian friends, inviting them to express their doubts.

Also, gather your youth with some of their faith-questioning friends so they can listen to you, and avoid the temptation to create a confrontational climate. Let everyone keep in mind that it will be a space not to force anyone to believe in something they don't believe in, but to better understand what their thoughts are about faith and to better understand ours. In fact, one of the best tactics to help someone realize their mistakes is to ask them questions: Some will probably have arguments against religions or refer to the bad testimonies of certain believers. Let them express themselves and don't defend the indefensible. And if the questions point to the historicity of certain biblical stories, don't try to prove them wrong but help them focus on what those stories mean. In this way, your young adults from the discipleship group will learn to answer not only their doubts but also those of others and they will be better prepared to give an account of what they believe.

If you think they are ready, give your young adults some responsibilities to participate in, but wisely assess each other's emotional and spiritual state. In fact, one possibility is that the first time you can be the one to lead the meeting, and then you can have other similar meetings but have some of the young adults lead, sharing what they have learned.

LESSON 5

SEXUAL INTELLIGENCE

It would be a shame if being able to make love, you only end up having sex.

Lucas Leys, *Different*

Sexuality touches all aspects of the human being since it is intimately linked to our identity, and for this reason it is such a sensitive subject.

Starting with the fact that a sexual act brings us to life; from then on, our perception and management of our sexuality will have a lot to do with the kind of disciples we will become. In childhood, sexuality begins with gender recognition, managing nudity, attachment to dad or mom, and the role we play as male or female. Preadolescence is marked by the appearance of secondary sexual characteristics. Adolescence and young adulthood bring major struggles, such as sexual attraction, falling in love, or even addictions such as pornography and masturbation, promiscuity, and other types of dangerous behaviors.

The continuous hyper-sexualization of social media has ended up instilling in us a conceptualization of sexuality that is only physical. Over and over again in both songs and movies, one will find messages of sex with love as the ideal; however, the subtext is quite the opposite, purporting that sex has nothing to do with love but is exclusively an animal attraction that arises from one's own attraction, need, and pleasure.

SEXUALITY WITHOUT INTELLIGENCE IS TOO HIGH A RISK.

We are facing a world that has despised true love, just as Jesus prophesied in Matthew 24:12 when he said: "There will be so much sin and wickedness that the love of many will grow cold." Indeed, the way in which society assumes the concepts related to sexuality allows us to see that genuine love has become blurred either in feelings or in carnal attraction, lowering the understanding of what love is to the most basic satisfaction of personal desires.

What do we as Christians do then? If we focus on fatalistic options, we risk giving the world the wrong image of the freedom we have in Christ. And if we take this subject lightly, we will succeed in disenchanting people with the gospel, especially young adults.

The expression "Sexual Intelligence" contains two words that are apparently unrelated to each other. However, today more than ever, we need to unite them. During young adulthood we must help our brain make decisions related to sexuality, because sexuality without intelligence is too high a risk.

✪ SEE YOUR ENVIRONMENT

Prepare and discuss a list of open-ended questions regarding society's thinking about sexuality. Some questions can be:

What is the difference between having sex and making love?

What are the most common messages about sexuality on social media?

How do you define good and bad in terms of sexuality?

Sometimes we can assume something isn't real simply because we haven't asked about it, so it's good to start here. A well-planned conversation can help your young adults feel confident to discuss these topics.

It will also help them to analyze the information that is usually disseminated by the media, and that is not always true.

Other, more personal questions that you can add are:

Can you talk openly about sex in your home?

Where did the information you received on this topic come from as a teenager?

Do you feel uncomfortable dealing with these types of issues?

End the meeting by thanking everyone for being open and honest in discussing this topic. Some young adults tend to keep these things to themselves while others will speak bluntly about their opinions, showing no mercy as they judge. Often these attitudes are indicative of feelings of guilt and shame attached to sexual issues, but can also be due to a variety of other reasons. Your job as a discipler is to help them continue to trust, listen without judging them, and give them the necessary tools so that they can get rid of the sins that plague them and begin to manage their sexuality in a more intelligent way.

TRAIN TOGETHER

Young adults today have been overexposed to sexual content that is distorted and false. Since childhood, they have seen suggestive images and ideas through many different venues including the internet, TV, movies, and even some video games.

What they were probably not exposed to is information about STDs (sexually transmitted diseases) and the emotional, psychosocial, and even spiritual consequences of having an STD. That's why it's important for you to talk about it.

You can add a few of these questions:

- What are the main STDs that exist in the world today?

- What are the STD statistics in our country?

The purpose of this lesson is not to be alarmist, nor is it for you to learn to deal with fear, but it is important that you know about this other side of reality. We won't accomplish much if we focus on instilling fear in our young adults so that they will stay away from unsafe sex. What we need is for them to make intelligent sexual decisions, understanding the very real risks of poor judgment in this area and the harm it can cause in their present and in their future. Now move on to the stories. As always in this second step of the STRIDE sequence, your personal testimony is very valuable, and you can also include other stories close to your context.

An interesting effect of the stories could be corroborated with the statistical consequence of the MTV series "16 and Pregnant." Some might suspect that the intention of the show was to de-glamorize the idea of getting pregnant in adolescence. But the fact that there was a statistical effect surprised a lot of people because a year after the series aired, teenage pregnancies began to drop in the United States.

And what about pornography? This word, which comes from the Greek *porneia*, has been translated in the Bible as "fornication," and refers to all forms of sexual immorality that are outside of God's design for sexuality. When you look at a pornographic photo or film, your mind takes a picture and stores it inside your brain, and the equation is simple: the more porn you see, the more photos stored in your mind, and don't think for one second that it won't affect you!

The following sequence can be observed in addiction to pornography:

1. The person views pornography, perhaps casually or out of curiosity.

2. An intentional search is initiated.

3. The search intensifies and the addiction begins, since the person finds it almost impossible to stop the search.

4. Insensitivity to soft porn arrives. The things that the person has seen no longer give them the same satisfaction as before, so they begin a search for new forms of pornography to feel that satisfaction again.

5. The brain is captive with actions of twisted sex that drive twisted desires. (This sequence is well known to those who produce pornography, and for this reason they play with fantasy.)

6. All this search for sexual sensations makes the person finally end up going to places or looking for people to make their fantasies come true.

The distance from the first glance to addiction and disorder is very short and fast; that is why it is important to warn our young adults about this process. As the addiction to pornography intensifies, the insensitivity toward others also intensifies because the brain begins to search wildly for self-satisfaction without considering any consequences. (For example, the well-being of the people involved in pornographic films, the objectifying and abuse of people in this realm as well as the resulting broken families.)

By contrast, we can now talk about pure and beautiful sexuality that God intended for two people to enjoy together in unadulterated authenticity. Clearly stated, when two people are intimate sexually with each other, they are sharing their deepest identity and the sexual act unites them far beyond that which is physical. This sharing is much more sublime when it is done in the safety of two people who are fully committed to each other for eternity. That is precisely marriage. (If your students haven't read the *Diferente* book yet, it would be great if they do so soon. As part of this class, you could have everyone read the *Sexo Espiritual* chapter the same week.)

RUMINATE ON A MODEL

JOSH McDOWELL

Josh McDowell is a christian speaker and writer of several books. His two most prominent themes have been sexuality and apologetics. McDowell was born in Michigan in 1939. He grew up conflicted, caused mainly by the mistreatment he received from his alcoholic father, which in turn affected his self-esteem. He was also negatively impacted by sexual abuse that he endured in his childhood and adolescence, which is recounted in the biopic *Unbreakable.*

Josh questioned the faith for many years, considering himself an atheist during his adolescence and part of his youth, to the point of deciding to prepare a thesis to refute the Christian faith with historical and scientific evidence. But God had other plans... and Josh turned to the gospel precisely because of the results of his own historical study on faith in Christ. With these same proofs he later studied theology, and thus he developed his apologetic arguments to defend the cause of Christ.

Many pastors, educators, and youth leaders have been influenced by Josh McDowell over the years, especially hearing him speak so bluntly about sexuality.

Josh McDowell developed his ability to write deep yet easy-to-understand details on a subject as complex as sexuality, while being honest about his own struggles.

He writes:

Your most powerful sexual organ is not covered by a bathing suit. The ultimate key to sex is not between your legs. It is between your ears. When it comes to sex, the magic happens in your brain.
Josh McDowell, *The Naked Truth*

📖 ILLUMINATE YOURSELF WITH THE TRUTH

The Word of God is a living instruction that guides the human being in all his ways and obviously, then, has a lot to say about the sexual realm.

Some classic passages about sexuality in the Bible are 1 Corinthians 6:12 and 1 Corinthians 10:23, which talk about the things that not good for us and, of course, there is also the vital text of 1 Corinthians 6:19, which talks of the body as a temple of the Holy Spirit. These texts on holiness and purity are fundamental, although there are others that are less well known. In the letter to the Hebrews, we find one of them:

THE GREATER AWARENESS WE HAVE OF GOD'S PATERNITY OVER OUR LIVES, THE LESS NEED TO SIN WE WILL HAVE.

Marriage should be honored by all, and the marriage bed kept pure, for God will judge the adulterer and all the sexually immoral.
Hebrews 13:4

Even if your young adults are single today, some of them will not be tomorrow, or at least they will start loving relationships and have responsibilities to take care of, and that is why these words are so vital.

Any act of sexual impurity that they commit prior to marriage will be dishonoring their marriage bed, and it is crucial to teach them that sexual addictions not overcome in youth will be carried into marriage. Bad habits, pornography, masturbation, sexual impurity, and everything that was not overcome in singleness will manifest itself in marriage in some way.

Another very important biblical passage is the following:

The one who does what is sinful is of the devil, because the devil has been sinning from the beginning. The reason the Son of God appeared was to destroy the devil's work. No one who is born of God will continue to sin, because God's seed remains in them; they cannot go on sinning, because they have been born of God.

1 John 3:8–9

What a strong text, right?

Christians sin, but we cannot be given over to sin. These are two different realities. If we are delivered to sin, that is, surrendered to it, it is because we did not understand the grace of God. It will destroy us if we don't trust his plan and will. It is essential that your youth understand this idea.

The key to this confidence is acquiring a deep sense of God's Fatherhood over our lives. This is what the passage refers to when it speaks of being "born of the Spirit" as Jesus explained it to Nicodemus in John chapter 3.

There is a powerful mystery in understanding the Fatherhood of God and his grace that decreases our propensity to sin. It is the miracle of gratitude and trust.

If we are grateful to God for his love of us and trust in his identity, our propensity will be to flee from sin.

And while it is true that we remain human, imperfect, and fallible, we must trust what Scripture says is real. The healthy Christian life is not about some isolated events that are either good or bad, but about the correct direction of our lives. It is a process in which the greater awareness we have of God's paternity over our lives, the less need to sin we will have.

What shall we say, then? Shall we go on sinning so that grace may increase? By no means! We are those who have died to sin; how can we live in it any longer?

Romans 6:1–2

🔒 DENY YOURSELF

Being dead to sin means not wanting it. It implies giving up all those temptations that we had previously allowed ourselves, and that now we will no longer allow. It requires putting our feelings and desires aside, to firmly hold the decision not to sin. It is a conscious act of intellect, added to the intelligent submission of the soul and emotions; a full exercise of our will, willing to submit to Christ.

WE MUST REFUSE TO FIGHT OUR SECRET SINS IN SECRET.

Author Neil Anderson writes in the book *A Way of Escape*: "God doesn't command us to do something we can't do, or the devil can stop us from doing. In Christ you have died to sin, and the devil can do nothing to you. He will tempt you, accuse you, and try to deceive you, but if sin reigns in your body, it is because you have allowed it to do so. You are responsible for your own attitudes and actions."

It is good not only to renounce sin but to fight against it. For that, the discipleship group also exists, and we must refuse to fight our secret sins in secret, resolving to encourage and take care of each other, confessing our struggles and failures so as to lift each other up.

🙌 EMULATE THE CALL

Some of the following activities could take you a week or two, or even up to a month. It depends on how far you want to go with the topic and the lesson. Remember that the need for your young adults to learn to make intelligent decisions regarding these issues is urgent and vital to their future.

Some activities that you can organize are:

- **Discussion on STDs.** Plan a discussion about sexually transmitted diseases. You can organize it with your young adults or join with other young adult groups from other churches. Invite a couple of Christian doctors whom you have interviewed before to find out what they believe and what their knowledge is about them. Look up some statistics about STDs in your country and in the world and write them on posters placed around the room. The idea is that young adults themselves can be part of a movement that seeks to promote purity and provide adequate information so that other young adults can make their decisions with sexual intelligence.

- **Panel of single parents.** Organize a panel with men and women who have become parents at an early age without being married. Preferably, look for adult leaders with a good testimony and whose story can be told. Ask them a series of questions that reveal how difficult their condition was. Talk about their relationship with their own parents, and the reasons why they believe this unplanned pregnancy came about. It will be an interesting opportunity for your young adults to have another look at the subject!

- **Conference about pornography.** Speak clearly with your youth about the risks of pornography and its consequences. Find some phrases from authors who talk about it. Maybe you could even invite a speaker or a ministry to give the talk. A well-known one is the Free in Christ ministry and perhaps you can find another similar one in your country or city. At the e625 Institute there is a refresher course about the scam of porn.

What every young disciple should remember as a result of this class is that:

- Sexuality goes beyond the physical dimension.

- God wants them to enjoy healthy sexuality.

- What they do with their bodies and minds today has consequences in the present and in the future for themselves and for other people.

- Although we sometimes give in to certain temptations, it is possible and vital to take care of the trajectory of our intentions and keep for purity.

- We are here to help each other walk in purity.

LESSON 6

CRUCIAL DECISIONS

When someone does not believe in their tomorrow, they do not find enough reasons to make good decisions in their present.

Lucas Leys, *Different*

It is in the stage of young adulthood where the most complex and transcendental decisions of life are usually made. Many of these decisions have the potential to change a person's future completely, which is why this discipleship project is all about helping young adults make the best decisions.

One of the big problems seen in many young adults today is the lack of ability to live their own lives. This can be noticed in many ways. Students who cannot finish their degree because they get distracted by their friends' agendas and end up moving away from the goal they set at the beginning. Young adults who believe everything they see on TV and live trying to impress people who will be inconsequential in their futures. Confused college students because their professors told them something they never thought about, and they end up giving up the faith because they allowed themselves to be convinced by atheist arguments without bothering to consider Christian arguments despite growing up in a church. Not to mention young adults who do not have a plan or at least a dream for their futures because they are very comfortable extending their adolescence.

A disciple of Jesus must be aware of their need to make good decisions at each stage of their life, and for this they must seek the appropriate options to reduce

THIS DISCIPLESHIP PROJECT IS ALL ABOUT HELPING YOUNG ADULTS MAKE THE BEST DECISIONS.

the risk of making mistakes in any of them. As disciplers, we have the power to help our youth to make wise decisions.

Although life has many important areas, there are three issues that are often critical for young adults: vocation, their partner, and financial decisions. Obviously, we could also include faith, but that decision is what the whole project is about, so in this lesson let's reflect on the other three decisions.

⬨ SEE YOUR ENVIRONMENT

Ask your young adults why they think so many young adults don't finish college and why marriage seems to be delayed in so many cases.

As a pastor or leader, you must know the reality of your congregation, but you can add the opinions of other pastors and leaders to have a broader picture of the reality of your environment regarding these issues.

What do the young adults of our churches think about...?

- marriage

- having kids

- choosing a career

- building a profession

- managing money

Have your young adults look at how men and women between the ages of 26 and 35 live in their environment. Send them out to talk with some of them, to explore their situations and motivations. Inquire about the following aspects:

- How many are married, and how many are single?

- Have they chosen a career, or have they built a profession?

- Are they satisfied with their decisions?

- Do they regret any of them?

- What is their position on the issues listed above?

- Is there a history of large debt in their family?

- What is their financial policy for handling credit cards?

Asking these questions can help your youth get a big picture of how adults feel about decisions they have made in the past. Looking at those who have already experienced what we will soon have to experience can be a great contribution, as it helps us to see the future more clearly and can be crucial to avoid mistakes that others have already made.

TRAIN TOGETHER

In the study "Economic Outlook for Latin America" carried out by the UN in collaboration with ECLAC, the Development Bank of Latin America, and the OECD, dropout rates in adolescence and youth generally exceed 50% of the population and in some countries reach up to 70%. The reasons are diverse, but the highest percentages are related to poverty, the use of alcohol and drugs, and early pregnancy. As for poverty, we know that many young adults are forced to look for a job or create some kind of business to help their families, or to be able to subsist independently, still the data is increasingly alarming regarding the use of alcohol and drugs. This behavior does not distinguish between wealthy people and people with limited resources. It simply undermines the person and their family, destroying all their goals and desires. Early pregnancy also affects the plans and future of the young adults involved since the arrival of a baby generates the need to work to support a home that is not sought or planned.

All this has to do with decisions. If we could get our children, adolescents, and young adults to learn to choose wisely, surely those rates would change.

WHAT OFTEN HAPPENS IN THE CHURCH IS THAT WE DEDICATE OURSELVES TO SOLVING PEOPLE'S PROBLEMS INSTEAD OF HELPING PREVENT THEM.

Learning to choose appropriately at each stage of life is critical since it can prevent us from innumerable problems. Unfortunately, what often happens in the church is that we dedicate ourselves to solving people's problems instead of helping prevent them.

Talk about your story and that of people close to you. Guiding young adults to make their decisions wisely is a difficult job because it is long-term and requires the constant attention of parents, teachers, and leaders. In our case, as children of God, we can ask him to help us in the challenging task of forming intelligent disciples.

RUMINATE ON A MODEL

GIOVANNI OLAYA AND VANESSA GARZÓN

Giovanni and Vanessa are married. He is an architect, although he is much better known as a rocker and vocalist for the Colombian band Pescao Vivo. She is a social communicator and professional model. Their story is an example of good decisions in life despite being exposed to many temptations. You can find it in the book *El rockero y la modelo que llegaron vírgenes al matrimonio* (The Rocker and The Model That Made it to Marriage as Virgins).

Being a professional model in such a difficult world was hard for Vanessa. She had to learn to live with the public exposure without losing her Christian convictions. She is one of those people who knows that she is a daughter of God before anything else. Early in her professional career she made the decision that she would not pose nude nor participate in campaigns that promoted alcohol or cigarettes. These are difficult decisions for someone who wants to dedicate herself to modeling, but they have undoubtedly been decisions that have helped her to safeguard her faith and her convictions.

Giovanni comes from a home in crisis. His mother was a church leader, to whom many went for advice, and he was one of those boys who grew up in the church and chose to continue that path, but this was not the case with his younger brother, Iván, who by that time was already immersed in the world of drugs. This was the catalyst that made Giovanni look for alternatives for his brother to hear the gospel, and he succeeded! After many years of effort and closed ears, finally the music that Giovanni created was what attracted his brother Iván and his friends to Jesus.

Vanessa and Giovanni had to go through various processes making difficult decisions. Choosing each other to commit to marriage was undoubtedly a key decision. When you make a decision like this, you are either ensuring a good future or putting it at risk.

On the other hand, considering the careers they had both chosen, it was clear that deciding to be a good testimonial would not be easy. In their book *The Rocker and The Model*, they describe in detail all the adventures they had to go through to keep their convictions intact and grow in their relationship with God. Vanessa recounts how she had to stand firm in her convictions when she was asked to pose nude or in skimpy bathing suits. Because of that attitude, many doors closed for her, but God opened others. And the decision of both of them to keep sexually pure until they got married is one of those decisions that you don't see people make very often anymore. Clearly, it's not every day that you meet couples like this. Still, there are many couples who, thanks to Vanessa and Giovanni's testimony, have made wise decisions for their lives, their futures, their sexuality, and their careers.

Do you know other similar testimonies?

How can you use the example of this or other couples to confront, inspire, or teach those you are discipling?

📖 ILLUMINATE YOURSELF WITH THE TRUTH

Solomon had the opportunity to ask God for whatever his mind imagined, and out of everything he could have asked for, he chose wisdom. From there, he had everything he wanted, although he still made some wrong decisions later, proving that we can never stop depending on God.

Look at this description.

> *King Solomon, however, loved many foreign women besides Pharaoh's daughter—Moabites, Ammonites, Edomites, Sidonians and Hittites. They were from nations about which the LORD had told the Israelites, "You must not intermarry with them, because they will surely turn your hearts after their gods." Nevertheless, Solomon held fast to them in love. He had seven hundred wives of royal birth and three hundred concubines, and his wives led him astray.*
> **1 Kings 11:1–3**

Solomon's equation was simple: lots of wives plus lots of trouble. The choice of a wife or a husband demands direction from God. Not because it is magical but because it is a matter of intelligent evaluation.

Some practical questions are:

Do this person and I share values? Which ones exactly?

Do we share the faith?

Do we share compatible life plans and projects?

In the light of the Bible, these questions must be answered wisely, and Solomon is a reminder that God's advice is better than any human criteria, no matter how wise we think we are.

Solomon chose his wives for political expediency, and probably sexual attraction as well, but this brought disastrous consequences for himself, his lineage, and an entire nation.

Many years later, Paul wrote:

> *Be very careful, then, how you live—not as unwise but as wise, making the most of every opportunity, because the days are evil. Therefore do not be foolish, but understand what the Lord's will is.*
> **Ephesians 5:15–17**

Wisdom and foolishness are two opposite attitudes. The first is a virtue, the second is a character flaw. Wisdom and full trust in the Lord will lead you to success, while foolishness will make you lose people, dreams, and opportunities.

What is a wise person like?

In the Word of God we can find true wisdom. The book of Proverbs is famous for giving us many pearls of wisdom. These are some of the characteristics that, according to this book, distinguish a wise person:

- **Knows how to listen**: The wise man is attentive to what God says in every aspect of life. He is also humble to listen to advice (Proverbs 4:10).

- **Knows how to discern**: The ability to distinguish between good and evil, from God's perspective, was given to human beings from the beginning of their creation. The serpent's trick was to make them think that they would be wise knowing everything without the need for God (Proverbs 1:7).

- **Knows how to receive correction**: God tells us that if we listen and heed his corrections, he will open his heart to us and pour out his Spirit on us, and he will make his thoughts known to us (Proverbs 1:22-23).

- **Knows how to stay quiet**: Usually, the first person to speak without thinking ends up messing up. A great act of wisdom is to always think before you speak and to know when it is better to say nothing at all (Proverbs 13:3).

- **Knows how to be humble**: Humility is a difficult quality to develop, but the one who achieves it reaches a significant level of maturity and wisdom (Proverbs 15:33).

- **Knows how to control their anger**: God's Word says that he who is easily angered is foolish, while he who is slow to anger is intelligent (Proverbs 14:29).

Read with your young adults the book of Proverbs. They can read all the chapters or focus on just two or three. Challenge them to use the same format to extract more wisdom principles like the ones listed above. It can take you a meeting, a day, a week, or a month. It depends on how much you want to develop this topic with them. The best part will then be helping them apply each of the principles they found to their daily lives. That is what being and making disciples of Christ is all about!

Finally, let's talk a bit about money management. It is perhaps the least under-stood area, even though it is a recurring theme in Scripture. For example, the par-able of the rich young man that we read in Matthew 19:16-23 tells us of Jesus's encounter with a young man whose heart was set on riches. A young person's attitude toward money will say a lot about their character. This story highlights the urgency of better training our youth in financial matters, both in managing their finances adn in discerning the state of their heart when it comes to money.

Dishonest money dwindles away, but whoever gathers money little by little makes it grow.
Proverbs 13:11

Perhaps church communities would not need to come up with creative ways to "motivate" people to be generous and give their offerings or tithes if we just taught the new generations the principles of the kingdom when it comes to the management of money and walk with them, helping them to fulfill those principles. Then we would have communities that are generous, focused on global mission, and not deep in debt or worried that the congregation cannot support its own pastor.

> **THE PAST CANNOT BE CHANGED, BUT IN THE PRESENT, WE DEFINE THE FUTURE.**

 DENY YOURSELF

The past cannot be changed, but in the present, we define the future. Around the age of 20 is the time to focus on the decisions that lie ahead, as each decision can turn your life toward a different tomorrow. Any path you take involves opening some doors and closing others. This is difficult for many who do not want to refuse anything, and therein lies their mistake. You must make decisions and pay the price of those decisions!

Here are some examples:

- If you choose to preserve your sexuality for marriage, you will need to stay away from anything that poses a risk. You will probably have to decide not to have a romantic partner for a while. And if you have a partner who is tempting or pushing you to take that step, you may have to make a drastic decision and cut off that relationship. Although temptation will always be there, with good accompaniment, mentoring and discipleship, and making the right decisions, you can preserve your sexual purity and save yourself until marriage.

- If you decide to live a life without pornography, great. At the same time, you must close any door that could encourage you to fall into that sin. Give up control of your privacy; let someone else help you with that. Give up using the internet alone, especially in your room at night. You can ask someone else to help you, and report to them from time to time on this.

- If you are going to finish your university degree, you cannot give up in the middle of the degree. Sometimes you will have to give up friend-ships, outings, or other things you enjoy doing, in order to spend more time on your studies.

- If you decide to get into a relationship, make sure beforehand that you both want the same things, that they think the same about marriage and children, and that you are both sure of what God has told each of you. Choosing this person well is key since this decision will influence the rest of your life!

- If you decide to take out a loan, carefully analyze your reasons. Evalu-ate if it is justified or not, if you will be able to pay it, and if you have planned well how to use of the economic resource you will receive.

Each choice is linked to leaving or giving up something, often even things that seem promising but are not suitable for us or right for this moment in our lives. We must refuse to make decisions without God's counsel.

🖐 EMULATE THE CALL

Share with your young adults this list of tips for making good decisions in the future:

1. **Redeem your past.** Your past can be a horror story and yet simultaneously be the best starting point for your success because it allows you to experience unique circumstances that others have not experienced. What did you learn? Heal what needs to be healed and use it as a springboard. As the saying goes, what doesn't kill you makes you stronger. Even consider the mistakes of your parents or other leaders in your life, not to fill you with resentment but to rebound and know that you are going to be different from them. You are not doomed to repeat anyone's mistakes. Not even yours.

2. **Ask God for direction.** Study his Word to know what God did in the past. Give time to prayer and seek the advice of wise people by reading good books that have to do with the decisions you have to make. God will whisper to you in those exercises.

3. **Surround yourself with good influences**. When looking for someone to ask for advice, think of mature people who can be reliable references and who have proven what they are telling you in their own lives. Remember, "Plans fail for lack of counsel, but with many advisers they succeed" (Proverbs 15:22).

4. **Accept correction.** This part is difficult for many young adults, but you should know that being corrected will help you avoid repeating the same mistakes and making new ones. Having someone above you who can correct you when you have taken a wrong step is vital for someone who is training for the future. "Listen to advice and accept discipline, and at the end you will be counted among the wise" (Proverbs 19:20).

5. **Challenge the future.** Most of the time, when bad decisions are made it is because the person is thinking only in the moment and not about the consequences that the decision will bring later. Taking a drug or not, choosing one friendship over another, and standing firm instead of running are all decisions that involve thinking about the future. Choosing a career or committing to a partner are also decisions that will inevitably

change the course of a person's life forever. Dream in HD and with the best picture and sound quality imaginable!

After sharing these tips, ask your young adults to list the most important decisions they will have to make in the next five years and discuss them, their implications, and their projections.

You can end this lesson by creating an "accountability pledge" so your young adults can count on you when making important decisions. As a discipler, you are in a position of great responsibility, and it is essential to commit to being accountable to someone else. We are all in this together!

LESSON 7

INFLUENCING IN SOCIETY

The world is not as it should be... it's broken, we broke it.
God personally intervened to begin his restoration project
and lay the foundations of his kingdom in Jesus.

Samuel Pagán and Alex Sampedro, *Creed*

Jesus invites each disciple to embrace his historical and social role in the environment in which we must develop. For this reason, we must learn to contextualize the message of the cross. The church and its disciples cannot be late and only react defensively to whatever is happening. In its dizzying progress, the world constantly tries to get ahead and leave us behind to react instead of taking preventative or transformative action to create the future. That is why developing disciples with a social conscience and an influential mindset is vital.

For too long, some circles of the church were enclosed in a bubble to avoid contamination, and thus some forgot that the function of the church was precisely to bring life and hope to this lost world.

We are the messengers entrusted with the ministry of reconciliation. Who should we reconcile? The world with Christ. How will we do it? By being an active part of the society in which we live.

⬟ SEE YOUR ENVIRONMENT

Send your youth out to look at the community they are a part of. You can analyze with them what percentage of the ministry is done outside the doors and differentiate it from the ministry done inside. Some examples include:

INSIDE MINISTRIES	OUTSIDE MINISTRIES
Worship, praise, dance	Evangelism
Services in the sanctuary	Short-term missions
Sunday school	Cell-groups or house churches
Bible classes	Conservatories
Prayer groups	Workshops for entrepreneurs
Youth groups	Conferences for businesspeople
Counseling	Transcultural ministries
Preaching and teaching	School or language tutoring

The list can be much larger, but the approach should be the same. The youth must weigh the amount of ministry done inside and compare it to that done outside. Remember that the column on the right implies that the work is done outside; if the workshops for entrepreneurs are only given to the congregation, it should go in the left column. Activities will only be considered "Outside" if they are intentionally marketed to people who do not regularly attend church.

The purpose of doing this is not to evaluate or judge those who make the decisions in the church, but to make the disciple see the reality of their ecclesial community and the possibility to improve some things. That is why the disciples and disciplers are here!

THE CHURCH AND ITS DISCIPLES CANNOT BE LATE AND ONLY REACT DEFENSIVELY TO WHATEVER IS HAPPENING.

Some tactical questions are:

- What does my ecclesial community do for its wider community, in its neighborhood or in its city?

- How do church programs respond to the needs of the people in the area?

- What does the ecclesial community do to impact its environment?

By the way, it would be interesting to know what the surrounding people think about this. If you were to ask the neighbors what they thought of the Christian church in their neighborhood, what would they say? Many times, all people have are complaints: "They always bother us with the noise of their sound equipment"; "Every Sunday, the nearby streets have traffic jams, and the neighborhood is filled with garbage when they have their meetings"; "They don't even say hello when they see us." Instead of positively impacting their environment, these congregations are doing the opposite.

TRAIN TOGETHER

The church is called to be salt and light. That is, to be influential. The purpose of salt is to influence the food to give it flavor and to preserve it so that it does not degrade quickly. The purpose of light is to help us walk, so we don't stumble. That is what the church should be: a living organism that brings light to society so that no one stumbles and a great family that can be an example for a community that needs to stop its decomposition process.

A MATURE CHURCH CAN MAKE MORE SOCIAL CHANGES THAN A CHRISTIAN PRESIDENT.

In some sectors of the church, we have already realized the need to send more children of God to key government spaces. Even some pastors have turned to a political career, which is sensational if God has called them to do it, although it is always a sensitive issue for institutional representation to be sought with questions of political vision. However, profound change will surely come from the new generations.

We can encourage our disciples to be protagonists, active not only in government endeavors but in organizations that promote cultural activities with Christian values, be it in universities and colleges or sports institutions. We aim to promote kingdom values from wherever the Father has placed us. A mature church can make more social changes than a Christian president.

Imagine Christ's church understanding that its function is to positively influence the world with the values of the kingdom of heaven, not from the perspective of religion, but from morality and ethics. It seems like a dream, right? Unfortunately, the church tends to be very closed in on itself in its meetings, courses, and classes. Although all of these are fine and necessary, let us not forget the second part, that of going out and turning the world upside down with the message of Christ and the values of his kingdom.

The other challenge we must face is the sudden changes of culture in which we operate. Everything changes so fast that when we finally have the answers to one dilemma, it is already over, and four worse ones have appeared.

Culture analysts estimate that our culture is reinventing itself
every three to five years.
Lucas Leys, *El mejor líder de la historia*
(The Greatest Leader of All Time)

We need to be alert to what is happening in the world. As disciples, we must read the Bible more, but also the news, to be aware of how society is turning toward a future of greater darkness, because that is exactly where we will turn on the light! We will not do this by saying that the best way to live is by what our religion teaches, but by living the truth in love and making them see how good the world can be on the side of the Creator.

> *We can generate works that only Christians can understand, using symbols without any relevance to society, or we can rescue concepts from culture to present Jesus.*
> **Alex Sampedro,** *Artesano* **(Craftsman)**

From this perspective, the difference between a believer and a disciple lies in the action before society, that is, in intentionally generating works that contribute something to this decadent culture. A believer will feel content with attending a service, receiving a weekly portion of God's Word, accepting advice from time to time, and even being an active part of different groups within the church community. A disciple is not satisfied with what

EVERYTHING CHANGES SO FAST THAT WHEN WE FINALLY HAVE THE ANSWERS TO ONE DILEMMA, IT IS ALREADY OVER, AND FOUR WORSE ONES HAVE APPEARED.

happens around a service or a group, but will use that group to go where the need is. More radical disciples are needed to take this step of faith with tangible works!

> *The price of lack of discipleship is high for those without Christ. It is also high for the poor people of this world.*
> **David Platt,** *Radical*

RUMINATE ON A MODEL

RICK WARREN

Saddleback Church in Lake Forest, California, started in a house, with a Bible study of just seven people and is now a community of thousands of members. What happened to make it grow so big? The answer is as simple as it is compelling: Rick Warren, its founder and former pastor, took the time to visit people in his community and ask them what the barriers were that prevented them from attending a church, and he solved them. Rick critically observed his community and gave effective responses to the problems that society presented around him.

His greatest impact, however, may not be that he has gained so many members for his congregation, but rather that he has been concerned with finding the best way to make each of them a constantly growing disciple, actively involved in the mission of extending the kingdom of heaven.

BEING LIGHT WHERE LIGHT ABOUNDS IS VERY EASY. BEING LIGHT WHERE THERE IS TREMENDOUS DARKNESS IS MUCH MORE DIFFICULT.

Warren looks beyond Sunday attendance or the success of his big initiatives. He has helped his members to positively influence society. Thinking like this has meant being invited as a speaker at the United Nations, the World Economic Forum, the African Union, various renowned universities, and different organizations that share his way of seeing the world. It would be great if many more ministers were called upon to advise governments and organizations globally.

One of the catalysts for exerting this influence on society has been the venture that Rick has titled "PEACE Plan." This plan is a humanitarian program that tries to reach 5 critical areas in the world, which Rick calls the Global Goliaths: spiritual emptiness, self-centered leadership, extreme poverty, pandemic diseases and illiteracy, and lack of education.

Some have criticized him for a lecture he gave to thousands of Muslims talking about working together to solve the social problems that plague the planet. I wish any of us could have such influence as to be heard by people of other religions, beliefs, political convictions, or social interests! Being light where light abounds is very easy. Being ligth where there is tremendous darkness is much more difficult.

📖 ILLUMINATE YOURSELF WITH THE TRUTH

The following is an important prayer of Jesus:

> *My prayer is not that you take them out of the world but that you protect them from the evil one.*
> **John 17:15**

John did well to record these words of our Lord. Perhaps he sensed that we were going to need them. The society of that time was going to hate the disciples of Jesus because they would bring light to live better, and for that reason they would suffer persecution. Jesus prayed then, asking for their protection from the evil one and asking the Father to not take them out of the world, since it is precisely to the world where they had been sent.

Today's disciples must also be clear that we will be judged and criticized if we try to help the world. A lost society is like a wounded dog: if a stranger comes to help it, it will most likely bite them. Hence, our message cannot consist only of words, good intentions and spirituality. It takes a great willingness to change what needs to be changed!

> *Do not merely listen to the word, and so deceive yourselves. Do what it says. Anyone who listens to the word but does not do what it says is like someone who looks at his face in a mirror and, after looking at himself, goes away and immediately forgets what he looks like.*
> **James 1:22–24**

As we read in this passage, if someone just listens to the Word without putting it into practice, they are deceiving themselves. Putting the Word of God into practice in all areas of our life makes us live in truth. His Word reminds us that we are his children, but also his servants and his warriors. We are ambassadors and have been called to reconcile the world with him:

> *That God was reconciling the world to himself in Christ, not counting people's sins against them. And he has committed to us the message of reconciliation. We are therefore Christ's ambassadors, as though God were making his appeal through us. We implore you on Christ's behalf: Be reconciled to God.*
>
> **2 Corinthians 5:19–20**

This task that has been entrusted to us obligates us to take that message to everyone, applying the truths of the Word to the needs of each culture. God bless the young adults who will venture into political science to transform society, the artists who will heal the contamination of the arts, and those who will decide to become educators because they know that in their hands, they will have the future of many! God bless the disciples who will be future lawyers, businessmen, economists... and all those who decide not to be just another member of a society that breaks day by day, but to be a gear that facilitates the union of the lost in a much greater plan, the plan of a God who is waiting for them and longs to embrace them as beloved children!

DENY YOURSELF

Considering what we are talking about and reading about in this lesson, it should be obvious that one of the sins that offends God is indulgence. Being comfortable in a religious bubble without being salt or light. Words without actions or believing without anyone outside noticing what our beliefs are, all this must be left behind.

Many different authors have proposed that there are seven areas of society that we as a church must affect: government, the arts, education, the family, the media, finances, and religion. As good disciplers, we must challenge the disciples to interfere in one or more of these areas to fulfill their work as disciples of Jesus influencing the environment. What offends God is not only disordered sexuality, or not going to the temple on the weekend, but also not being the salt and light that he commanded us to be. Therefore, we must deny any spirit of comfort, cowardice, or indifference.

EMULATE THE CALL

Make a visual diagram with the areas of conquest mentioned in the previous point and add some like "sports" or remove some and then ask your young adults to think of ways to affect change in each of those areas. Then ask at least three of them to share their personal perspective or inclination toward one of those areas. Help them to overcome their fears and their justifications, and direct them toward the fulfillment of God's purpose for their lives.

LESSON 8

UNFINISHED BUSINESS FROM THE PAST

To forgive is to free a prisoner and discover that the prisoner was you.

Lewis B. Smedes, *Forgive and Forget*

Carrying all the circumstances that we have experienced and that have not been fully resolved can bring instability, incorrect behavior, and problems in interpersonal relationships to our lives. A broken relationship, abuse, abandonment, an excessively controlling mother, or a tyrannical father are all examples of experiences that create emotional predispositions that need to be healed.

Let's picture a tree. Jesus said that a good tree bears good fruit. A bad tree cannot bear good fruit, and we can certainly know the tree by its fruit. Christ compares our life to a tree with roots, a trunk, branches, and fruit. We will have to try to repair the roots (what we lived in the past) to produce good fruit (in the future).

Likewise, every good tree bears good fruit, but a bad tree bears bad fruit. A good tree cannot bear bad fruit, and a bad tree cannot bear good fruit. Every tree that does not bear good fruit is cut down and thrown into the fire. Thus, by their fruit you will recognize them.
Matthew 7:17-20

NOT DEALING WITH UNFINISHED BUSINESS FROM THE PAST MAKES OUR ROOTS DRY UP, AND OUR BEINGS WITHER.

A person is known by their actions; those are the fruits. But all actions have an origin; they come from somewhere. The source of the fruit is in the root. And the roots are our past. If the roots are good, the fruit will be good, but if the roots are contaminated, the fruit will be similarly tainted. That is why it is so important to heal the roots.

Jesus was paraphrasing Psalm 1 since the same comparison is made there between a person and a tree, giving us more specific characteristics:

> *Blessed is the one who does not walk in step with the wicked or stand in the way that sinners take or sit in the company of mockers, but whose delight is in the law of the LORD, and who meditates on his law day and night. That person is like a tree planted by streams of water, which yields its fruit in season and whose leaf does not wither whatever they do prospers.*
> **Psalm 1:1–3**

This passage contains the beautiful promise that if we follow God's advice, we will be like trees planted near a river, with our roots (the past) in contact with the waters. If we do so, we will constantly bear fruit and never wither, for we will be healthy in the heart. The figure of the waters is related to the Word of God and healing. Something similar is mentioned in Revelation 22, where it says that there will come a day when we have access to the tree of life, which will constantly bear fruit and whose leaves will be for the healing of the nations. Not dealing with unfinished business from the past makes our roots dry up and our beings wither. Therefore, in this part of the discipleship process, we will enter an essential stage: heart healing.

SEE YOUR ENVIRONMENT

Unless you believe there is an unsafe situation, encourage your young adults to talk seriously with their parents about the past. The idea is to be able to face certain "ghosts," since parents and older siblings have some answers to interpret better the events we have experienced.

Keep in mind that it will not be easy for some of them to talk about bad memories or wounds since this can open up emotions stored since childhood. For this reason, you must personally accompany each disciple to support them, especially if they have to confront something genuinely dark.

The principle is that there are some wounds that we can't forget and that it is good to talk about them and solve them with forgiveness.

TRAIN TOGETHER

There are two broad categories to healing in each person's past:

1. The mistakes, the bad decisions, or the damage we caused to others.

2. The sins that others committed against us (offenses; harassment; abuse; all forms of physical, psychological, or sexual violence; scams; disappointments; etc.).

Both categories are very personal. You must touch on them carefully as a group and also personally.

On the other hand, there are several problems that can appear in a person's life related to the past and the lack of a healthy heart:

- **Unforgiveness** occurs when we have received an offense or grievance and we have not forgiven the one who committed it. The pain this produces hardens the heart and can spark anger, rage, resentment, or even hatred.

- **The root of bitterness** has to do with a spiritual condition in which a person's life stops being sweet and becomes bitter, difficult to enjoy. This can transform someone who is a fighter and hard worker into a pessimistic and defeated person.

- **Abandonment, bullying, and lack of acceptance** can produce in the person feelings of rejection that will stop them in their path of growth.

- **Blaming** their lives on some mistake from the past or a bad decision can cause a feeling of weight and remorse that does not allow the person to enjoy the freedom they have in Christ.

- **Fear** of facing different situations in life is also something that stops people. Fear of death, failure, marriage, and facing problems can cause serious consequences and even lead the person to a spiritual paralysis.

- **Shame** may come from episodes that included emotional grievances or ridicule from others. This can cause reactions of shyness, cowardice, fear of speaking in public, or difficulties in relating. It can also cause anxiety and distress.

Some people have the conviction that upon reaching the feet of Christ, and putting faith in him, it is no longer necessary to talk about anything from the past. What we must differentiate is that everything about the past has been forgiven by God, but not necessarily by that person.

Many live a silent suffering that they carry day by day, and despite having come to Christ, their wounds still need to be treated. It is not that Jesus's sacrifice was not enough, but sometimes the wounds are so strong that they leave emotional scars that we need to deal with in a special way. It is for this reason that we need to dig deeper to explore the biblical principles that will allow us to experience true freedom in Jesus. Our Savior many times addressed those who, despite believing in God, were somehow blinded from seeing what ailed them.

The Spirit of the Sovereign LORD is on me, because the LORD has anointed me to proclaim good news to the poor. He has sent me to bind up the brokenhearted, to proclaim freedom for the captives and release from darkness for the prisoners, to proclaim the year of the LORD's favor and the day of vengeance of our God, to comfort all who mourn, and provide for those who grieve in Zion to bestow on them a crown of beauty instead of ashes, the oil of joy instead of mourning, and a garment of praise instead of a spirit of despair. They will be called oaks of righteousness, a planting of the LORD for the display of his splendor.

Isaiah 61:1–3

One day Jesus read this portion of the prophet Isaiah in the synagogue, and then announced that this Scripture had been fulfilled at that moment in their midst. If we read carefully, we see that there he speaks of the need for good news to reach the poor, and that consolation will reach the afflicted and bring freedom to the prisoners. Thanks to Jesus, the hour of compassion has arrived for those who cry, beauty instead of ashes, and jubilation instead of tears! He was speaking to people who did believe in God, by inheritance and by conviction; and he told them that in him

CHRIST PROMISES US THAT NO WOUND PLACED IN HIS HANDS WILL REMAIN THE SAME.

they would have all this and would finally be like oaks, trees of justice, vigorous and slender.

You can have Christ in your heart and still be hurt. That is why Christ promises us that no wound placed in his hands will remain the same. He is the tree of life that brings healing to the nations.

RUMINATE ON A MODEL

NICK VUJICIC

Nick Vujicic was born without arms or legs; it is obvious that no one would want to be born like this. And while everyone admires Nick's tenacity to get ahead and overcome all obstacles in life, we must know that this path has not been easy for him.

OUR PAST DOES NOT DEFINE US FOREVER, AND NO CIRCUMSTANCE CAN PREVENT US FROM BEING WHAT WE HAVE BEEN DESTINED TO BE.

Having to face criticism and mockery for his condition, not being able to easily adapt to all environments, and not being able to do the things that other people do, were all reasons why Nick no longer wanted to continue living. So he had to struggle with the desire to kill himself, with depression, and with completely justified anger. Isn't it understandable that Nick would be angry with the world and even with God for having to live in such a way?

It was the presence of his parents, and their intentional accompanying him and helping him to rise above the difficulties that this condition meant for him that helped Nick to change his way of thinking and, consequently, completely change what was once a miserable life to become an abundant life. If there is someone who could complain about life, it would be him. But he decided to stop feeling sorry for himself. Nick decided to get up and start being the person he was meant to be. He learned to eat by himself, to move from one place to another, and even to swim. All things that are everyday occurrences for us were an enormous challenge for him

Today Nick is a motivational speaker, writer, preacher, and consultant, touching the hearts of thousands of young adults who have once experienced rejection by the world. Nick is an example that we don't need everything to be perfect to grow and fulfill our purpose. A living proof that our past does not define us forever, and no circumstance can prevent us from being what we have been destined to be.

📖 ILLUMINATE YOURSELF WITH THE TRUTH

According to the Bible, forgiveness touches every corner of the heart. Forgiveness can restore relationships, remove emotional burdens, and free us from a soul prison that limits and holds us back.

Paul wrote:

> *Be kind and compassionate to one another, forgiving each other, just as in Christ God forgave you.*
> **Ephesians 4:32**

Many of the verses of Scripture that deal with forgiveness compare the act of forgiving others to the forgiveness we have received from God. Matthew 6:14; Colossians 3:13; Luke 6:37; and Mark 11:25 all speak of the same thing. How can it be that we have received so much forgiveness and cannot offer it to others? This probably has to do with the feeling that we have lost something. When someone offends us, they somehow rob us. They steal our peace or integrity, and produce in us a sense of loss, because the one who offended us "came out winning." And it is true that when someone offends us, they take something from us, but we must be aware that it is something that we can never get back. Not even maintaining a lifetime of hatred and resentment against that person will make us recover what we feel we have lost!

Jesus told us the following parable to teach us about forgiveness:

> *Therefore, the kingdom of heaven is like a king who wanted to settle accounts with his servants. As he began the settlement, a man who owed him ten thousand bags of gold was brought to him. Since he was not able to pay, the master ordered that he and his wife and his children and all that he had be sold to repay the debt.*

At this the servant fell on his knees before him. "Be patient with me," he begged, "and I will pay back everything." The servant's master took pity on him, canceled the debt and let him go.

But when that servant went out, he found one of his fellow servants who owed him a hundred silver coins. He grabbed him and began to choke him. "Pay back what you owe me!" he demanded.

His fellow servant fell to his knees and begged him, "Be patient with me, and I will pay it back."

But he refused. Instead, he went off and had the man thrown into prison until he could pay the debt. When the other servants saw what had happened, they were outraged and went and told their master everything that had happened.

Then the master called the servant in. "You wicked servant," he said, "I canceled all that debt of yours because you begged me to. Shouldn't you have had mercy on your fellow servant just as I had on you?" In anger his master handed him over to the jailers to be tortured, until he should pay back all he owed.

This is how my heavenly Father will treat each of you unless you forgive your brother or sister from your heart.

Matthew 18:23–35

We received God's forgiveness by grace. It was a debt that has been dispensed to us. However, paradoxically, we are not always capable of forgiving those who have offended us, as we feel that they owe us a debt. We even come to think that the person should come to us to ask for forgiveness, and that only then might we think about forgiving him. But this is not what Jesus teaches. Forgiving others is a key mandate to live in freedom. If one does not forgive, they place the other in a prison, just as it happened in the parable that Jesus told.

But that prison is a cell in which both the offended and the offender will remain locked up with the other forever. That is why it is necessary to forgive, to free the other, yes, but also to be able to free yourself!

The Bible contains so much wisdom and we use it so sparingly! If we only followed the advice of Scripture with greater conviction, we would see the truth of things, the truth of our inner being, the truth of our thoughts... and knowing that truth would make us truly free!

There is, for example, a passage in Proverbs that tells us that forgiveness is an act of love. To not forgive is to insist on the offense, and that attitude can separate even the best of friends:

> *Whoever would foster love covers over an offense, but whoever repeats the matter separates close friends.*
> **Proverbs 17:9**

Forgiveness should be seen as an act of obedience and, at the same time, of love! Of obedience, because Scripture puts it in the form of a command, not a suggestion, and even warns us that forgiving brings a consequence: "Forgive, and you will be forgiven" (Luke 6:37). Of love, because it is a quality inherent to God that we, as his children, must manifest.

FORGIVENESS SHOULD BE SEEN AS AN ACT OF OBEDIENCE AND, AT THE SAME TIME, OF LOVE!

> *You, Lord, are forgiving and good, abounding in love to all who call to you.*
> **Psalm 86:5**

He forgives us because he is good and loves us, and we show that we love him by obeying his commandments and being like him in everything. In this case, by forgiving others.

🔒 DENY YOURSELF

There are several attitudes that we must decide to abandon in order to truly experience the healing and freedom that Christ offers us. (There are even things we could do with good intentions.) Here are some examples:

- **Justification of offenders.** To avoid the need to deal with certain painful issues for the soul, we usually raise arguments to justify those who have hurt or offended us: "It's been a long time"; "They didn't do it on purpose"; "Why open old wounds?"; "It is no longer necessary to talk about it"... Justification can, apparently, save us from problems, but it will prevent true healing.

- **Pride.** Some phrases that pride introduces into the mind are: "I don't need to deal with these things"; "I have lived like this for many years, and I will be able to continue doing it"; "I could forgive, but I don't want to talk about it"; etc. Pride hardens the heart so that the pain of the past is not so strong. It's an emotional self-defense strategy, but it prevents us from being completely healthy.

- **Comfort.** Some people force themselves to be okay. Many have even gotten used to answering that they are fine even when they are not, because they do not want to bring more chaos into their lives. They think that stirring up those waters will only bring them discomfort, and for this reason they choose not to say or do anything. The problem is that in this way they are condemning themselves to continue living with that weight.

- **Resentment and hate**. These are different attitudes that people often develop to deal with pain. As if repeating to oneself things like: "I'm never going to forgive them"; "I won't do them that favor"; or "I'd rather die than let that person win"; could be the answer for a heart that is looking for a way to better bear pain. The truth is that none of them help.

- **Anger.** Reactions of anger or rage are normal when there is a wounded heart. It's like that stray dog that is full of wounds and that, if someone comes close, bites them away. Reacting with anger and rage is a way of taking revenge against the world for that evil we have received. The problem is that these attitudes do not solve anything, and our hearts continue to be as much or even more hurt than before.

Clearly, none of these attitudes are wise. None will help us to heal the soul from the wounds of the past and, on the contrary, they are reactions that will increase the weight we carry day by day. As disciples of Christ, if we seek to be obedient to his Word, we need to give up these attitudes, refusing to have control over our feelings and giving up thinking that we can carry this weight alone. Denying ourselves means turning control over to God, surrendering to him, and freeing ourselves from the burden that weighed down on us. It implies recognizing that we do not need to defend ourselves because we have someone to defend us and, above all, someone to heal us.

You can guide your young adults to say a prayer in this way:

"Dear Father, today I admit that pride has gotten me nowhere and that I don't need it. I recognize that I have harbored grudges, resentment, and hatred in my heart, but I don't want to do it anymore. Starting today, I will stop justifying my offenders, I forgive them with all my heart. I let go of the pride that has hardened my soul, and I decide to be sensitive to your voice. I move away from all comfort that has stagnated me in my spiritual life. I take full responsibility for my actions in the past and ask your forgiveness for each of the wrong decisions I made, even if they were reactions to other people's sins. Starting today I leave in front of you this suitcase full of useless weight, so that you can take care of it. I rest in you. Amen."

🙌 EMULATE THE CALL

Forgiveness is one of the most sublime Christian disciplines. It is what God does, and it is what we must do. Forgiving does not mean justifying anyone, but freeing ourselves from those actions controlling us through the emotions they produce.

To close out this lesson, create a list of desirable future actions when faced with rejection or even abuse, because in this fallen world there will continue to be circumstances that young adults will face again at some point even though they are no longer children.

LESSON 9

SPIRITUAL NARCISSISM

The path of transformation is a painstaking and patient course of trial and error; it's a persistent and daily struggle.

Patrick Morley, *The Man in the Mirror*

The word "narcissism" comes from Greek mythology and has to do with Narcissus, who was a very handsome young man whose life revolved around himself; he considered himself superior to others in everything. Historically, the figure of Narcissus has been used as a reference to someone who only thinks of themself and everything they say, think, and do has to start with "I."

In the spiritual realm, we could say that a "spiritual narcissist" is someone whose life revolves around what he or she can receive from God and others, and who believes that church and ministry are there to meet their personal needs. Sure, no one is going to say this out loud, but attitudes like this can infect us all, making it a topic for a memorable discipleship lesson.

Spiritual narcissism, then, is the cultural inertia that pushes us to look at everything, including faith, through the lens of our exclusive convenience. Probably all of us at some point in our Christian life go through a stage like this, but we should not let it last too long.

SEE YOUR ENVIRONMENT

Tell your young adults about the Narcissus story and ask them what a modern-day spiritual narcissist would do. Allow them to share their ideas, and then add the following to the list:

- They pray every morning that everything goes well for them and that everything goes according to what they have planned.

- The complain to God for what they have asked for and have not received.

- They do not ask for others, since they cannot see the needs of others.

- They think that others should serve them, open the door for them, sing to help them worship, preach the Word, etc.

- They don't serve because they don't have time; their schedule is filled with many things that take them away from service in any form.

- If they do choose to serve, as some spiritual narcissists do, they serve to get something in return, such as recognition or admiration.

- They never focus on what God asks them to do, but rather on what they ask God to do.

Compare the list with what they said, and I'm sure they'll come up with a few more things.

TRAIN TOGETHER

The true gospel has much more to do with giving than receiving. It requires giving up things, rather than asking for them. It implies dying to rise again. If you look closely, the gospel of the kingdom of heaven that Christ preached and lived is the exact opposite of what we commonly think of in the world. Christ taught that to win, you must lose; to live, you must die; and to enter the kingdom, you must be like children. He also said that the last will be the first and that to be a leader, you must first be the one who serves everyone.

This is the time to talk about your own struggles with this issue. Remember that the problem is narcissism and not one specific person.

The gospel was not designed to supply our own needs. That sometimes happens in addition, but God's idea is not that we go looking for him to receive his favors or that we behave like good children to have the right to receive everything we ask for. In contrast to the list we made to describe a spiritual narcissist, following is a list of the attitudes that the Bible teaches as correct for a disciple of Christ.

IT'S NOT ABOUT HOW MANY FAVORS WE RECEIVE FROM GOD, BUT ABOUT HOW WILLING WE ARE TO LIVE A LIFE ACCORDING TO HIS WILL.

A disciple of Christ:

- Prays that God's will be accomplished in and through their life.

- Acknowledges God's sovereignty when they don't receive something they asked for.

- Is used to asking for others, praying for those in need, and even blessing those who have wronged them.

- Forgives those who have offended them and protects their mouth from curse words.

- Is convinced that serving others is the best way to love God.

- Finds time to serve God despite their many activities, and they enjoy it.

- Remains humble, even if they have reached a high-level position or rank and does not aim for recognition and admiration.

- Always asks God before making decisions and submits to his perfect will manifested in his Word.

As long as our decisions are focused on satisfying our own desires, we will be spiritual narcissists. If we want to stop being one, we must understand that the Christian life is not about how many favors we receive from God but about how willing we are to lead a life according to his will.

RUMINATE ON A MODEL

OSCAR SCHINDLER

The famous film *Schindler's List* shows the life of Oscar Schindler who became famous thanks to the enormous number of Jews he was able to save through his factories at the time of the Holocaust (the killing of millions of Jews during what we know of as WWII). The systematic extermination of European Jews was, for the Nazi party, the "Final Solution" or Endlösung. This film, based on the book *Schindler's Ark* by Thomas Keneally, describes the events that revolved around the change of mentality of Oscar Schindler who, initially blinded by his personal interests, joins the Nazi party in search of wealth or benefits. Thus begins his munitions factory, which is greatly improved by the war. The question is, how did a man of his condition, of good social position, and with the recognition and favor of the Nazi party, of which he was a part, suddenly decided to change his mentality to become a concealer and savior of so many Jews? What happened to that selfish, ambitious, greedy man, who sought his personal benefit in everything he did, that would turn him into the kind of hero who would be willing to give his life for others?

There may be many speculations about that, but most likely what happened is that God touched his heart. Among the multiple divine purposes evidently was the salvation of those 1,200 Jews (and of all their descendants, who to this day thank him for their lives). Oscar Schindler was the tool God used for that purpose, and in doing so he became a historical example that anyone can change their mentality and learn to think of others.

The most shocking thing is that this man decided to confront his own party, his compatriots and friends, his people... and all to defend a group of strangers! In the middle of a world war, he faced one of the most bloodthirsty armies in history, risking his own life, to hide this group of people who had nowhere to turn or anything with which to thank him.

This should make us think to what extent we should change our mindset so that we can see the surrounding reality in a different way. Surely God has already been speaking to the hearts of many, showing us a portion of the world's need so we would do something. We do not need a war to defend an

WE NEED LESS SELFISHNESS AND MORE COMPASSION.

entire people. We don't need a factory or a lot of money to serve the world. What we need is to love God above all things, and our neighbor as ourselves. We need less selfishness and more compassion.

📖 ILLUMINATE YOURSELF WITH THE TRUTH

Jesus denounced spiritual narcissism with this parable:

> To some who were confident of their own righteousness and looked down on everyone else, Jesus told this parable: "Two men went up to the temple to pray, one a Pharisee and the other a tax collector. The Pharisee stood by himself and prayed: 'God, I thank you that I am not like other people—robbers, evildoers, adulterers—or even like this tax collector. I fast twice a week and give a tenth of all I get.'
> "But the tax collector stood at a distance. He would not even look up to heaven, but beat his breast and said, 'God, have mercy on me, a sinner.'

"I tell you that this man, rather than the other, went home justified before God. For all those who exalt themselves will be humbled, and those who humble themselves will be exalted."
Luke 18:9-14

When Jesus told this story, he described very well the attitude of a spiritual narcissist with the example of the Pharisee. For this person, giving thanks had to do with putting others down and feeling superior, particularly pointing fingers at the tax collector. It must be considered that at that time tax collectors were frowned upon among the people of Israel, since their work was in favor of the Roman Empire. The taxes they collected impoverished their Hebrew brothers and enriched Rome. Thus, the contrast between these two people was impressive.

The Pharisee, who should have been the person most aware of who God is, and therefore should have walked in humility, lifted himself up! He considered himself to be better than others, judged, and thought that fasting, tithing, and keeping certain aspects of the law were enough to stand right before God and make him worthy of admiration. He never considered the attitude of his heart. Certainly, this man was a spiritual narcissist!

By contrast, the tax collector was hated by his own people and despised by the Romans. But he was sure of his condition as a sinner, to the point of not being able to even raise his eyes to heaven because he felt unworthy of the Father's favors.

For the people who heard this allegory from the mouth of Jesus, it must have been a shock. Jesus spoke well of someone they judged to be evil, and he spoke ill of someone they considered a spiritual authority. However, Jesus' intention was not to confuse people but to teach them to see beyond appearances. One person may keep many aspects of God's law for the wrong reasons, while another may have the right attitude in his heart even though others judge him to be evil.

Jesus presents here a spiritual principle that is inexorably fulfilled. He who exalts himself will at some point be humbled, while he who acknowledges his condition as a sinner and humbles himself before God, will be exalted in due time.

Also look at this passage in Philippians:

> *Do nothing out of selfish ambition or vain conceit. Rather, in humility value others above yourselves, not looking to your own interests but each of you to the interests of the others.*
> *In your relationships with one another, have the same mindset as Christ Jesus: Who, being in very nature God, did not consider equality with God something to be used to his own advantage; rather, he made himself nothing by taking the very nature of a servant, being made in human likeness. And being found in appearance as a man, he humbled himself by becoming obedient to death even death on a cross!*
> **Philippians 2:3-8**

In this case, Paul recommends to the Philippians that they be attentive to this kind of attitude. Pride, arrogance, and haughtiness are the kind of attitudes that cannot be easily seen in oneself. Recognizing that we are moving out of selfishness or vanity is not an easy thing! Here it seems that we are repeating what was said in chapter 3 about the challenge of character, but everything is related. Pride is a subtle and accurate weapon of the enemy, who seeks to make us believe that we are better than others.

Paul's instruction on this is clear: we should seek not only our own good, but the good of others. Let's watch at every moment what the intentions of our hearts are!

🔒 DENY YOURSELF

The story of Jesus is not that of someone who becomes great after being small, a nobody who becomes powerful, or someone who prospers after being poor. His story is the opposite. He is the one who, having everything, decided to leave it to serve.

What are we willing to give up to serve others?

EMULATE THE CALL

To close this lesson, encourage your young adults to tell a little about what each one imagines doing in the future, and then ask them this question:

What will you do to avoid narcissism in that future?

What will become evident is that it is vital to think of others and to sensitize our hearts through service. Here are some ideas to make it easier for you to think of others:

- **A social work trip.** Visit a nursing home, an orphanage, centers for young adults with different problems, or other social work entities. These types of activities will help your young adults to develop a social sensitivity and burden for those who suffer the most. After a first visit, some of your young adults may want to commit to providing more regular help to one of these institutions.

- **A family day.** Find a family that is going through an economic crisis. It can be from the same congregation that you attend (giving priority to the family of faith), although it can also be someone who is not a believer. Take food offerings or think of other needs that could be met for this family through this initiative.

- **Recycling campaigns.** Thinking about the environment can help some to stop thinking about their own condition and motivate them to take care of the planet. By doing this, we are changing the culture that surrounds us. This is not just a campaign, but it should become a new lifestyle. That is managing well what God gave us to take care of!

- **Support for animal shelters.** Sites that house stray dogs or cats often need a lot of help, and your youth can help there, collaborating by bringing toys or other objects or donating a few hours to help the people who work there.

- **Personal burdens.** You can ask your young adults to think of someone for whom they feel a special burden, someone they're worried about because they're going through a difficult situation, or just someone they'd like to help. Encourage your young adults to set aside time each week, or every other week, to spend time with this person and help them with whatever they need. This can also be the kickoff for these disciples to start discipling others!

Let's help those we are discipling to overcome that constant desire for consumption in our society today. It is not very useful to believe if our faith is not manifested in tangible works on behalf of others.

LESSON 10

THE CALL TO DISCIPLE

Discipleship is expensive because it costs life, and it is grace because it provides the only true life. It is costly because it condemns sin, and grace because it justifies the sinner. Above all, it is costly because it cost God the life of his Son.

Dietrich Bonhoeffer, *The Cost of Discipleship*

One of the greatest sins of the church is the number of Christians who are unaware of their call to discipleship. The concern in this regard grows when we see that the percentage of young adults who abandon the Christian faith after turning eighteen is very high, and still increasing.

It is essential, then, to offer a series of tools through discipleship that can be useful to our young adults in their daily battle to defend Christ and what they believe in. Above all, they need to enthusiastically take up their personal call to evangelism and to the multiplication of disciples.

All Christians must understand that the church's growth is every Christian's task.

⬡ SEE YOUR ENVIRONMENT

The Engel Scale is a model that was developed by James F. Engel, in which he proposes to place each person on a scale based on their degree of closeness or commitment to Jesus and his gospel. This is an attempt to represent the steps that a person normally follows in their knowledge of God, to be able to go little by little, overcoming the different barriers of each stage. The objective is not to go around giving Christians scores, but to help each person from their own context to take a step further in their relationship with the Lord.

This scale can be a very useful tool. Starting with a better understanding of where the person is now, we will have a better chance of helping them take the necessary steps to advance in maturity.

On the internet you can find the original scale as presented by James Engel, or you can use the following adaptation:

+5	Thinks, acts, and lives like Jesus most of the time (maturity)
+4	Helps others grow in Christ (whole faith)
+3	Takes steps of obedience (spiritual faith)
+2	Is instructed in the Word and knowledge of God (intellectual faith)
+1	Their heart has been captivated by their experiences with God (emotional faith)
0	**Makes the decision to follow Jesus (conversion)**
−1	Understands that they need God
−2	Sympathizes with the things of God although does not think they need him
−3	Is open to God as one of many spiritual resources
−4	Is indifferent to God
−5	Is totally against God

Level 0 includes everyone who has decided to follow Christ. From there upward are the positive numbers, which mark a development in the person's walk of faith. Downward are the negative numbers, which indicate a greater distance from God.

If we start looking at the scale from the bottom, levels -5 and -4 denote a greater degree of distance from God, to the point of being directly against him. Possibly at these levels the barriers are too high to try to convince the person of what we believe in. In these stages, testimony, genuine friendship, and letting them know that we are ready to answer any questions they have regarding spiritual issues are most useful. To deal with these levels, it is necessary to have an open and mature mindset. Traditional evangelism methods are usually not helpful, and even more often than not end up taking a person further away from God.

At levels -3, -2, and -1 we find people who are a little more open to faith, but with many questions, misconceptions, and other barriers that prevent them from truly knowing Christ. This is where we need to be ready to answer any questions people may have (the concepts in this chapter will most likely work best for these and higher stages).

Starting at level 0, and from there upward, we are already on a path of discipleship. In fact, surely your young adults are at one of those levels! It would be convenient, then, for you to be able to identify as clearly as possible where exactly each one is on the scale; that will give you a good guideline on how to continue walking with them to help them reach greater maturity in Christ.

🏘 TRAIN TOGETHER

In order to multiply our disciples and help them become the extraordinary Christian leaders that they can become, it is good that your young adults know some of the ideas and philosophical beliefs with which they will be confronted. In particular, conceptions about God such as the following:

- **Atheism.** This position defends that there is no deity. The term "atheist" comes etymologically from the Latin *athêus*, and this is derived in turn from a Greek word that literally means "without god(s)." The latest international study conducted by Gallup in 57 countries showed that, on average, 13% of their populations identify as atheist. (You can look up this and other facts on Wikipedia; see the article titled "Demographics of Atheism.")

- **Agnosticism.** This position denies the possibility that as human beings we have the capacity and real arguments to affirm or deny the existence of a god, and that it is impossible to have any certainty on the matter. The word "agnostic," from its etymological root, means "without knowledge." Agnostics do not believe in a god, although they do not claim to not believe in one either; that is, they neither deny it nor endorse it. British biologist Thomas Henry Huxley was the one who coined this term in the year 1869, and from then on many have adhered to this position. Charles Darwin, for example, claimed to be an agnostic.

- **Deism.** This position is open to the belief in the existence of a god or gods, but does not believe in the practice of any specific religion. In addition, a deist believes that, although there is a god who has been responsible for all creation, he does not get involved or interact with it. For this reason, a deist would not accept any manifestation from any god, nor any divine message, revelation, miracle, prophecy, or any statement that is supposed to come from a god.

- **Theism.** Unlike deism, theism believes in the existence of a creator god and attributes to him the possibility of intervening with the created work. Not only that, but this god would be committed to overseeing and governing his creation. From here various positions are derived:

  ◊ Monotheism. Believes in the existence of only one god.

◊ Henotheism. Believes that there are several gods, but worships only one.

◊ Kathenotheism. Believes that there are several gods, but one should be worshiped at a time.

◊ Polytheism. Believes that there are several gods and all of them are to be worshiped.

◊ Pantheism. Affirms that "all that exists is god, and god is all that exists."

(You can look up more information about this on Wikipedia under the heading "Theism.")

- **Secular humanism.** This position proposes to discard all religious beliefs and instead places science and technology as the only mechanism for improving the human condition in all its dimensions. It denies everything supernatural, affirms that morality is an achievable goal without including God in the equation, and maintains that issues regarding the government must be handled from a secular perspective. This philosophy is the one that prevails today in educational systems around the world.

After learning (or remembering) these concepts, it is worth analyzing where we stand and what exactly we believe.

We say that we are monotheists because we believe in the existence of a single God who is the creator of the universe and sovereign over it. Monotheism is a branch of theism so in that sense, we are theists.

However, some believers, despite being aligned with Christianity, claim that there are no supernatural manifestations, and that it is most likely that God is not involved with his creation. They would perhaps fit more within the position of deism.

In the branch of deism, we could also think of locating those who claim to be believers in God but do not accept the idea of the church, of living and growing in community; for them it is just an individual belief.

Now, regarding the issue of henotheism vs. monotheism, when studying the Bible, sometimes it seems that the text admits that there are other gods. Take, for example, these passages:

> *Do not worship any other god, for the Lord, whose name is Jealous, is a jealous God.*
> **Exodus 34:14**

> *For great is the Lord and most worthy of praise; he is to be feared above all gods.*
> **Psalm 96:4**

> *Give thanks to the God of gods. His love endures forever.*
> **Psalm 136:2**

Also remember Jesus saying that we cannot serve two masters (gods) and using the word *mammon* to refer to the god of wealth (in the original Greek of Matthew 6:24).

Even Satan is called "the god of this age."

> *The god of this age has blinded the minds of unbelievers, so that they cannot see the light of the gospel that displays the glory of Christ, who is the image of God.*
> **2 Corinthians 4:4**

However, we must keep in mind that when the Bible refers to these "gods," also called "idols" in some passages, it is referring to forces, things, animals, or people to whom men assigned the character of deity. In biblical times it was common for peoples to "raise" gods and worship them. Pay attention to the verb "raise," because in theology there are always two directions —from top to bottom, and from bottom to top— and the difference is very important. When Scripture speaks of other gods, it does not refer to other spiritual beings equivalent to God, but to statues or images made by human hands, which men treat as if they are gods, making them worthy of their trust and prostrating themselves before them. In other words, giving them the honor that only belongs to the one true God.

In Scripture we find many passages that mention these "gods" or "idols" made by men. Look at these examples:

> *For all the gods of the nations are idols, but the LORD made the heavens.*
> **Psalms 96:5**

> *It is true, LORD, that the Assyrian kings have laid waste all these peoples and their lands. They have thrown their gods into the fire and destroyed them, for they were not gods but only wood and stone, fashioned by human hands. Now, LORD our God, deliver us from his hand, so that all the kingdoms of the earth may know that you, LORD, are the only God.*
> **Isaiah 37:18–20**

The idols mentioned in the Bible are not spiritual beings less than God. They are images or statues made by the hands of men, which the people treat as gods. We could also include here those who assign a deity to angels, or to Satan himself, as is the case with satanists.

Perhaps some believe that this type of reflection is useless, but it is important to instruct our disciples even in these questions that seem "merely theological." God's revelation to us is progressive, and those who do not advance or go deeper into what they believe could get stuck in the dynamics of religion and think that it is enough to have believed and to be part of a church and share its practices. The reality is that our human mind is incapable of fathoming the totality of God. Therefore, we can never think that we know everything. On the contrary, every day we must strive to continue knowing God more and more. That's what a disciple does!

Your young adults should fall in love with talking about the true God and living like Jesus. And in making that commitment, they must continually be intentional about infecting others with that faith and lifestyle.

RUMINATE ON A MODEL

CLIVE STAPLES LEWIS

It is true that C. S. Lewis has been recognized worldwide for his literary career and his contributions as a professor. Yet possibly one of the greatest contributions that the church has received from him is the book *Mere Christianity*, in which he reflects his perspective as an apologist. It is always interesting to hear the story of someone who initially called himself an atheist or agnostic, as is the case with Lewis, and who later converted to Christianity. His conversion, like that of many atheists, implied a previous period of struggle against God, during which he was filled with arguments to accuse the divine figure of falsehood and to maintain himself far from faith. The wonderful thing is that it was precisely that battle, that search against God, that brought Lewis closer to God.

They say that, like Saul, C. S. Lewis was a persecutor of the church, and after his encounter with Christ he became its defender. There are two amazing things about C. S. Lewis: First, his ability to manifest Christ through the literary art that God placed in his hands, and to reach the world in creative and unusual ways, often misunderstood by those who judge everything from the perspective of what religion suits you. Second, that he was not satisfied with his first literary writings but decided to write several works that speak openly about the faith. Who among us could achieve this? Being as efficient and successful in any field enough to be listened to by the whole world, and to be able to talk about Christ in any field, to make ourselves heard, and to become someone whose criteria is highly valued by others... It would be good for us to read some of his work! We could start with *The Chronicles of Narnia*, but probably we will obtain much more fruit if we study his book *Mere Christianity*, and even better if we can analyze the theological reflections in his satirical work *Screwtape Letters*.

It is important to reflect on what should really be the goal of the disciple. We must know the world from various perspectives, be aware of the arguments of atheism and agnosticism, defend our faith with important reflections, and use not only faith alone but all expressions of the arts and sciences to confirm the existence, wisdom, and power of God. But, above all these things, we must live out that faith in our own flesh, because it would be useless to have a reference like C. S. Lewis if the magic of his stories and writings were not evident in his life. Reflecting Christ in our lives is the real goal.

GENUINE FAITH IS NOT BLIND.

📖 ILLUMINATE YOURSELF WITH THE TRUTH

Genuine faith is not blind, and your young adults should know this text by heart:

> *Now faith is confidence in what we hope for and assurance about what we do not see.*
> **Hebrews 11:1**

If you pay attention to the broader context of this text, you will see that the entire chapter of Hebrews 11 tells us about people who trusted God's promises. That is, disciples. Although they preceded Jesus's incarnation, they trusted God and his promises, and that includes his great promise of the coming Messiah.

Part of our faith is understanding that we are to be prepared to share it and answer any questions from those who are not yet disciples. Look what Peter says:

> *But in your hearts revere Christ as Lord. Always be prepared to give an answer to everyone who asks you to give the reason for the hope that you have. But do this with gentleness and respect, keeping a clear conscience,*

so that those who speak maliciously against your good behavior in Christ may be ashamed of their slander.
1 Peter 3:15–16

Paul says this to his disciple Timothy:

But as for you, continue in what you have learned and have become convinced of, because you know those from whom you learned it, and how from infancy you have known the Holy Scriptures, which are able to make you wise for salvation through faith in Christ Jesus. All Scripture is God-breathed and is useful for teaching, rebuking, correcting and training in righteousness, so that the servant of God may be thoroughly equipped for every good work.
2 Timothy 3:14–17

And we can end with Jesus himself defining the mission:

"Come, follow me," Jesus said, "and I will send you out to fish for people."
Mark 1:17

Then Jesus came to them and said, "All authority in heaven and on earth has been given to me. Therefore go and make disciples of all nations, baptizing them in the name of the Father and of the Son and of the Holy Spirit, and teaching them to obey everything I have commanded you. And surely I am with you always, to the very end of the age."
Matthew 28:18–20

DENY YOURSELF

To think that leadership, evangelism, and discipleship are only to be done by others is one of the worst tragedies of Christianity.

The call to influence others with the way, the truth, and the life is for every born-again Christian, and perhaps the greatest temptation for every modern Christian is not vices or sexual immorality, but to live a boring Christianity, of just going to the sanctuary without ever multiplying ourselves in others.

 EMULATE THE CALL

Challenge your young adults to prepare for a future of evangelism.

Recommend the following books to learn doctrine from the nuance of evangelism and discipleship:

- *Credo* [Creed] (Samuel Pagán y Alex Sampedro)

- *Reasonable Faith* (William Lane Craig)

- *Making Sense of God* (Timothy Keller)

- *Mere Christianity* (C. S. Lewis)

- *Artesano* [Craftsman] (Alex Sampedro)

> **THE CALL TO INFLUENCE OTHERS IN THE WAY, THE TRUTH, AND THE LIFE IS FOR EVERY BORN-AGAIN CHRISTIAN.**

We always have people around us to evangelize and disciple. Encourage your young adults to start right now with at least three people they can start praying for.

Meditate on these principles:

- **Relational discipleship.** Discipleship may include a program (like this book) but its essence is close relationships.

- **Evangelism and discipleship go hand in hand**. True evangelism is not reduced to just an explanation about the cross but uses that as a starting point to make the cross a way of life.

- **New generations.** The church is always one generation away from extinction, and we can be models and sow fertile ground by evangelizing and discipling those who are younger.

- **Trust that the Holy Spirit will complete the good work.** By sharing the gospel and teaching the Word of God, the result is the fruit of the Holy Spirit and the faith of people. We only water with love, and that is why Paul gives us this promise:

Being confident of this, that he who began a good work in you will carry it on to completion until the day of Christ Jesus.
Philippians 1:6

BIBLIOGRAPHY

- **Anderson, Neil.** *Una vía de escape* (A Way of Escape). Miami, Florida. Editorial Unilit. 1995.

- **Craig, William Lan**e. *Fe razonable* (Reasonable Faith). Salem, Oregon. Publicaciones Kerigma. 2017.

- **George, Jim.** *Un joven conforme al corazón de Dios* (A Young Man After God's Own Heart). Grand Rapids, Michigan. Editorial Portavoz. 2014.

- **Kinnaman, David.** *Me perdieron* (You Lost Me). Miami, Florida. Editorial Vida. 2013.

- **Leys, Lucas.** *Diferente* (Diferent). Miami, Florida. Editorial Vida. 2015.

- **Leys, Lucas.** *El mejor líder de la historia* (The Best Leader In History). Miami, Florida. Editorial Vida. 2012.

- **Leys, Lucas.** *Liderazgo Generacional* (Generational Leadership). Dallas, Texas. Editorial e625. 2017.

- **Leys, Lucas.** *Stamina.* Editorial Dallas, Texas. e625. 2019.

- **Leys, Lucas and Jim Burns.** *El código de la pureza* (The Code of Purity). Miami, Florida. Editorial Vida. 2012.

- **Mancini, Will.** *Iglesia única* (Unique Church). Miami, Florida. Editorial Vida. 2014.

- **McDowell, Josh.** *Evidencia que exige un veredicto* (Evidence That Demands A Verdict). Miami, Florida. Editorial Vida. 1982.

- **McDowell, Josh.** *La verdad desnuda* (The Naked Truth). Weston, Florida. Editorial Patmos. 2011.

- **Meyer, Joyce.** *Belleza en lugar de cenizas* (Beauty Instead Of Ashes). Miami, Florida. Editorial Unilit. 1994.

- **Morley, Patrick.** *El hombre frente al espejo* (The Man In Front Of The Mirror). Miami, Florida. Editorial Vida. 2007.

- **Pagán, Samuel/Sampedro, Alex.** *Credo* (Creed). Dallas, Texas. Editorial e625. 2018.

- **Platt, David.** *Radical* (Radical). Miami, Florida. Editorial Unilit. 2012.

- **Plaza, Héctor.** *El carácter del líder* (The Character Of The Leader). San Vicente, Ecuador. 2018.

- **Sampedro, Alex.** *Artesano* (Craftsman). Dallas, Texas. Editorial e625. 2018.

- **Ortiz, Félix.** *Cada joven necesita un mentor* (Every Young Person Needs A Mentor). Dallas, Texas. Editorial e625. 2017.

- **Ortiz, Félix.** *Valores* (Values). Dallas, Texas. Editorial e625. 2019.

MY NOTES

MY NOTES

MY NOTES

MY NOTES

MY NOTES

MY NOTES

MY NOTES

SOME QUESTIONS YOU SHOULD ANSWER:

WHO IS BEHIND THIS BOOK?
Especialidades 625 is a team of pastors and servants from different countries, different denominations, different church sizes and styles, that love Christ and the new generations.

e625.com

WHAT IS E625.COM ABOUT?
Our passion is to help families and churches in Latin America to find good materials and resources for discipleship of the new generations and that is why our website serves parents, pastors, teachers, and leaders in general 365 days a year through www.e625.com with free resources.

ZONA DE CONTENIDO
PREMIUM

WHAT IS PREMIUM SERVICE?
In addition to reflections and free short materials, we have a service of lessons, series, research, online books, and audiovisual resources to facilitate your task. Your church can access this service per congregation with a monthly subscription that allows all the leaders of a local church to download materials to share as a team and make the necessary copies that they find relevant for the different activities of the congregation or their families.

CAN I EQUIP MYSELF WITH YOUR HELP?
It would be a privilege to help you and with that objective we have our events and our possibilities of formal education. Visit www.e625.com/Eventos to find out about our seminars and go www.institutoE625.com to learn about the online courses offered by Instituto e6.25

DO YOU WANT CONTINUOUS UPDATES?
Register right now for e625.com updates depending on your field of work: children, preteens, teens, young adults.

LET'S LEARN TOGETHER!

e625.com

🅕 🅣 🅞 ▶ /e625COM

Downloads
Subscription

Recursos
gratis

Store

Chat

Magazine

INSTITUTO
e625

Online Education
www.institutoe625.com

Events

Seminars

Books

e625.com